THE SACRED SYMBOLS OF MU

THE SACRED SYMBOLS OF MU

BY
COL. JAMES CHURCHWARD

ILLUSTRATED

AUTHOR OF THE MU SERIES

THE LOST CONTINENT OF MU
THE CHILDREN OF MU
COSMIC FORCES OF MU, VOLUME ONE
COSMIC FORCES OF MU, VOLUME TWO

BE, BOOKS
ALBUQUERQUE
THE C.W. DANIEL COMPANY LIMITED
SAFFRON WALDEN

A BE, Books / The C.W. Daniel Company Ltd. Co-Publication

Printing History

THE SACRED SYMBOLS OF MU

First Published in 1933 © James Churchward
Published in England by Neville Spearman Ltd., 1960
Published by Warner Books/Paperback Library, New York, 1968
Co-Published by BE, Books/The C.W. Daniel Company Ltd., 1988
Reprinted © 1992

ISBN 0-914732-24-2
BE, Books c/o Brotherhood of Life, Inc.
110 Dartmouth SE, Albuquerque, NM 87106 ◆ U.S.A.

—— & ——

ISBN 0-85207-198-1
The C.W. Daniel Company Ltd.
1 Church Path, Saffron Walden
ESSEX CB10 1JP ◆ U.K.

Cover Art: "The Sacred Symbols of Mu" © 1987 Jeffrey K. Bedrick

PRINTED IN THE UNITED STATES OF AMERICA

PRINTED WITH SOY INK ON RECYCLED PAPER

This book is dedicated to
MARJORIE V. LEA HUDSON
whose high ideals are the Four Great Virtues
as inscribed in the Sacred Inspired
Writings of Mu

1988 Edition
Dedicated to
NORMAN PAULSEN
Whose book *Christ Consciousness*
is recommend reading

CONTENTS

LIST OF ILLUSTRATIONS

LIST OF ILLUSTRATIONS

PREFACE

This work on Sacred Symbols has been compiled at the suggestion of the late Irving Putnam who felt and assured me that such a work would be appreciated by the public.

The kindly way in which the public have received my first two books on Mu calls for my most sincere thanks and makes me feel that my life's work has not been in vain.

In this work I have given my *personal* view why religion is in such a chaotic state today. There are over three hundred religions and sects and only *One God*.

J. C.

THE SACRED SYMBOLS OF MU

CHAPTER I

INTRODUCTION

I WISH particularly to point out in the present volume that I am not giving the meanings of symbols in the vestments in which they are now garbed. I am giving *their origin* and *original meanings.*

Up to the time of Mu's submersion all symbols retained their original meanings. From the time of Mu's destruction I must pass over about 5,000 or 6,000 years. Those were years when seemingly no history was written except a few scraps in India and Egypt.

During this time mankind apparently was reviving and repeopling the earth, after its almost total destruction by the submersion of Mu and other lands and the subsequent formation of gas belts and mountains.

On entering Egypt 6,000 years ago we find that many of the original symbols had survived but were very much Egyptianized, especially in pattern or design, with an incomprehensible theology attached to them. A multitude of new ones had besides been added, most of them having esoteric or hidden meanings.

This confusion increased when Upper and Lower Egypt merged into one kingdom. The two peoples not only commingled personally, but also their two sets of symbols. Thus two sets were made into one without any being discarded. It meant at least two symbols for every conception. So great was the confusion of symbols in Egypt, 4,000 to 5,000 years ago, that hardly one-half of the priesthood understood those used in the temples of other cities, although they might be but a few miles away.

The next period to note in Egyptian history is the reigns of the Ptolemys.

Many Greek philosophers then went to Egypt and were taught the Egyptian Sacred Mysteries. This knowledge they took back to Greece, commencing about 600 B. C. In Greece the Sacred Mysteries were Grecianized, new names and further theology were added. The result, generally, was the creation of amusing myths. The familiar Grecian myths may therefore be said to be influenced by the legends and teachings of Egypt and India.

The next point to note is Mu's destruction, which removed her motherly control over religion and science throughout the world. The consequence was that each colony framed its own laws, at the same time making changes in religion to suit themselves.

It is very noticeable among all ancient people that directly the control of the Motherland was removed, those countries began to fall back. As time went on they so degenerated in science and religion that the teachings of the First Great Civilization were at last entirely forgotten and became a thing of the past. Myths, those shadows of the past, alone remained. Here and there, however, solitary flowers strove to raise their heads out of the weeds which now choked the world's garden.

Coming down to present times, I find writers, supposed to be scholars, giving meanings to symbols that are purely mythical, the outcome, it may be, of fantastic dreams, and absolutely erroneous. Where they got their ideas I cannot imagine. Certainly not from the ancient writings. The result is that science has drifted into an age of theories. Theories are made subservient to facts. A fact cannot be a fact unless their crazy theories prove it. The more abstruse and bizarre the theory is, the more, apparently, it is scientifically thought of. A theory that is not even understood by the originator himself, and by no one else on earth, meets with scientific approval.

SYMBOLS AND FREE MASONRY.—Freemasons in their ceremonies use many of the ancient symbols. They freely admit that the original meanings are now forgotten but they know that originally the symbols were sacred, being used in religious ceremonies in the infinite days that are past and had a religious and moral meaning in line with the First Religion of Man—their origin.

Symbols and symbolisms are a principal division of archaeology. I am not a professional archaeologist, but I love the ancient and for over fifty years have been diligent in the study of it. When Mu went down the school of archaeology went with her.

ARCHAEOLOGY.—The date when archaeology was first studied reaches far back into the distant past. More than 15,000 years ago, the ancients had special colleges for its study.

In these colleges a very profound knowledge of their past was attained. The further we go back, the more profound we find that archaeological knowledge.

Like all other ancient sciences, archaeology had a dark cloud cast over it when Mu the Motherland sank and the First Great Civilization was wiped out. Only seeds, remnants of mankind, were left here and there, out of which a new civilization was in time to develop.

It is virtually within memory of living man that the study of archaeology has been again undertaken. Those who today call themselves archaeologists are, generally, diggers of the remains of man who lived, say, from 1,000 to 5,000 years ago. These are but of yesterday in human history. Why do they not go back to the beginning, as the ancients did 15,000 years ago? The archaeological study of the ancients included the whole history of man from his beginning 200,000 years before, if the astronomical evidence whereby such dates are computed may be accepted.

Archaeology embraces much more than it is thought to do. As the ancients studied it, it was a fascinating story. It may be deemed a religion for, at every step, the student is confronted with works of a Supreme Conception, with symbols of the power and wisdom of the Creator. The sights cause him contemplation, contemplation brings him in touch with the Supreme, the great Architect and Builder of all. As the student progresses, he becomes aware that other branches of science are intimately connected with it: geology, chemistry, astronomy and the Cosmic Forces. These must all be mastered to obtain the full benefit of what has been written and left behind by our forefathers for us, to act as guideposts to the greater knowledge.

NATURE.—Nature shows man what is the Origin of Life. It shows man's connection with the Great Source and the Great Cosmic Forces which control the Universe.

It also shows the origin of these Forces. Thus archaeology is but one letter in the long word that unfolds the wonders and glories of Creation, it brings man in closer touch with the Heavenly Father.

Again, incidentally, it shows that true science is the twin sister of religion: they are inseparable for without religion man could not comprehend the Cosmic Forces, and without fully comprehending these Forces he could not approach the Great Divine Love which rules the Universe.

The first chapters of the Bible were intended to teach man the workings of these Cosmic Forces. They failed to do so however because of the mistranslations of the Mosiac writings, which were in the tongue and characters of the Motherland, and were copies of the Sacred

Writings of Mu that Moses expounded when he was High Priest of the temple at Sinai. The esoteric temple writings of Egypt related the cause of the Flood, showing what the phenomenon actually was. Whoever wrote these chapters, as we now have them, failed *fully* to understand the ancient form of writing, as present man fails *fully* to understand the symbols and symbolisms which were there correctly copied.

The early part of the Bible therefore has not *fully* carried out the purpose for which it was intended. The Bible Moses actually handed down was the *Sacred and Inspired Writings, the greatest and most profound work ever penned by man, containing a science beyond the conception of present man.* Nothing however is, it seems, forever lost: for in various parts of the earth writings are being recovered which, when put together, provide us with a great part of the *Original Sacred Inspired Writings of Mu.* That which has been recovered gives:

The account of Creation down to and including the Creation of man and of woman.

The movements of all celestial bodies throughout the Universe, the Forces that are controlling their movement and the Source of these Forces.

The Origin of Life and what Life is, with the cause of the necessary changes in types of life during the earth's development.

Various geological phenomena and what their causes were.

And there is, finally, the coping stone of the Earth: *Man*.

I find a word frequently occurs in the Bible which is misapplied. I refer to "Miracle." There are no miracles. What seem miraculous is due to our ignorance. They are phenomena produced by the exercising of man's own Spiritual Force, given him at his creation. The Sacred Writings say that this Force was given to man *"to enable him to rule the earth."* Masters used their Spiritual Forces. Their works, not being understood by the multitude, were looked upon as miracles. "Master" was an ancient title bestowed on those who had mastered the use of their Spiritual Forces.

Those who spend their time merely in unearthing objects of the ancients are not true archaeologists. They are only diggers or miners. The archaeologist *reads* what he finds written on stone and clay, and informs the public what they say. A stone or plaque of clay with writing on it is only a stone or dried mud, having no more value than any other curious stone until the inscription upon it is read. Then it becomes a page of written history and may be the means of revolutionizing the thought and teachings of present man.

The value of archaeology is in this *reading*—thereby one gains a knowledge of the past. A voice is constantly calling, "Go forth unto nature and learn her great truths and lessons." Nature is the great schoolhouse for higher learning. No authorities are found there to muddle us. Nature is *the one and only authority*.

Every old rock, with its crinkly weathered face, every fossil, has its tale to tell; every leaf on tree and shrub whispers a story. The Universe, with its countless celestial bodies moving in perfect order and time, calls for observation and inspires a yearning to know the Source of all. All of these lessons are to be learned from nature to enable man in this life on the earth to prepare himself for the next step in his everlasting life.

THE ORIGIN OF RELIGION.—What is Religion? Max Müller says: "Religion is a mental faculty which, independent of, nay, in spite of sense and reason, enables man to apprehend the Infinite under different names and under varying disguises. Without that faculty no religion, not even the worship of idols and fetishes, would be possible, and if we will but listen attentively we can hear in all religions a groaning of the Spirit, a struggle to conceive the inconceivable, to utter the unutterable, a longing after the Infinite, *a love of God.*

"As soon as we know anything of the thoughts of man and his feelings, we find him in possession of a religion.

"The intention of religion, wherever we find it, is always holy. However imperfect a religion may be, it always places the human soul in the presence of God, and however imperfect and however childish the conception of God may be, it always expresses the highest ideal of perfection which the human soul, for the time being, can reach and grasp."

The period in man's history which Max Müller here

refers to is geologically known at the Pleistocene Period, coming after the submersion of Mu. Therefore what he found were shadows of the Sacred Inspired Religion of the Motherland, orally transmitted from father to son for thousands of years among the descendants of the remnants saved when the mountains went up and cataclysmic waves of water flooded the low-lying lands. This is corroborated in a paragraph where he says:

"There was a primitive Aryan religion, a primitive Semitic religion and a primitive Tauranian religion *before each of these primeval races was broken up and became separate* in language, worship and national sentiment.

"The highest god received the same name in the ancient mythology of India, Greece, Italy and Germany, and was retained by them. The name was Dyaus in Sanscrit; Zeus in Greek; Jovis in Latin; and Tiu in German (Wotan?). They bring before us all the vividness of an event which we witnessed but yesterday.

"The ancestors of the whole Aryan race, thousands of years it may be before Homer or the Veda, worshipped an unseen being under the selfsame name, the name of Light and Sky. Let us not turn away and say that this was, after all, but nature worship and idolatry. No, it was not meant for that, though it may have been degraded into that in later times. Dyaus did not mean the blue sky nor simply the sky personified; it was meant for something else. We have in the Veda the invocation 'Dyaus Pitar,' the Greek 'Zue Pater' and the Latin 'Jupitar,' and that means in these three languages what it meant *before these three languages were torn asunder: 'Heaven Father.'* "

Let us go back to the time when these languages were still one. In the Sacred Inspired Writings of Mu 70,-000 years ago the deity is frequently designated as "Heavenly Father" and "Father in Heaven." This name is more frequently used there than any other. Religion itself was based on the Fatherhood of God and the brotherhood of man. Being so prominent in the ancient writings, it is no wonder that it has persisted through the ages. Jesus, whose teachings were purely those of the First Religion, begins The Lord's Prayer with "Our Father which art in Heaven."

Besides quoting Max Müller I shall give a few extracts from writers on the subject whom science calls authorities.

Kant and Schiller both assert that "A myth does not represent a debasement, or a sinking down from original perfection, not a victory of sensuality over reason, but on the contrary, it manifests the advancement of a man from a state of comparative rudeness to freedom and civilization."

I am not in accord with these ideas because common reasoning tells me the case should be reversed. Fully ninety-nine per cent of the myths are traceable to legends. Legends are history orally handed down. History is a record of facts, so that myths instead of "manifesting advancement" manifest a retrogression; for they show that history, a part of civilization, is being forgotten. Therefore that civilization has declined.

Taylor, in "Anthropology," says, "In one sense every religion is a true religion. The great question which forced itself on their minds was one that *we*, with *our knowledge,* cannot half answer—what the life is which is sometimes with us but not always."

Taylor might with advantage consult the North American Indian, the semi-civilized Polynesians, the Maoris, the South African savages, and, beyond all, the Teachings of Jesus. The savages and semi-savages do not claim great knowledge on the subject. I have, however, found that they possess great wisdom which is untrammelled by the Queen of Myths, known as Science.

De Brosses says, "All nations had to begin with fetishes, to be followed afterwards by Polytheism and Monotheism."

I suspect De Brosses of toying with theories of our Simian origin. They have upset everyone who has ever come in contact with them. However, we shall let it pass because such writers as Max Muller, Dr. Happell, and Professor Pfliderer are directly opposed to such assumptions.

Hereafter, when dealing with the beginnings of religion, I shall show that man started with monotheism and it was only after Mu's destruction that there was polytheism and idolatry was practiced. The next quotation is as extraordinary:

"At a very remote period in the civilization of Egypt, Babylon, Mexico and Peru, the Sun God had *gained supremacy* as *the first* and *greatest of gods.*"

This is contradicted by all ancient writings. The Sun was never looked upon as a god by the ancients *but as a symbol only* of the Deity. Therefore, it was never worshipped by them. The sun, from the beginning, was the *monotheistic symbol* of the Deity. Being the monotheistic or collective symbol of the Deity, it was esteemed the most sacred of all sacred symbols.

This monotheistic symbol of the Deity existed tens of thousands of years before man settled in either Egypt, Babylon, Mexico or Peru. How, therefore, could it have gained supremacy *during their time?*

CHAPTER II

RELIGIONS

MU'S RELIGION.—It is fairly well established that all religions have a common origin. Let us see what that source was.

The first records of religion are more than 70,000 years old. They tell us that a body of trained masters from Mu, called Naacals, were carrying to her various colonies and colonial empires copies of the Motherland's Sacred Inspired Religion. These Naacals formed in each country colleges for the teaching of the priestcraft religion, and the sciences. The priesthoods that were formed in these colleges in turn taught the people. There is a very interesting ancient writing about the Chaldis, as the colleges were called in Babylonia. It says: "Everyone was welcome, be he prince or slave. Directly they passed into the temple, they were equal, for they stood in the presence of the Heavenly Father, the Father of them all, and here they became brothers in fact. No payment was charged; all was free."

Throughout the colonies and colonial empires these teachings were known as the Sacred Mysteries, a name that has persisted down to the present. In the

Orient they were also called the Books of the Golden Age. In later times, I find among Maya and Egyptian writings that the Sacred Mysteries were only entrusted to the high priesthood and the heir apparent to the throne.

Clement of Alexandria wrote: "The Sacred Mysteries are only entrusted to high priests and the heir apparent to the throne." This I find was not exactly true. Many of the Greek Philosophers who went to Egypt were entrusted with the Sacred Mysteries, among them being Solon, Plato, Pythagoras and Thales.

From various Naacal writings, sometimes called Neferit, and translations of the Sacred Inspired Writings, I shall try to outline the First Religion and show how it was taught to primitive man.

Religion started at a very early period in man's history; evidently when he could not understand anything that was abstrusely expressed. Apparently it was found necessary for explanation to use object lessons, symbols, where sight would supply the absence of words. I find the earliest symbols were of an elementary character, plain lines and simple geometrical figures. I refer to a date prior to 70,000 years ago, for according to the records man was so far advanced at that time that he was mastering the most intricate vignettes, tableaux, et cetera, which today puzzle our great scientists.

Evidently religion was originally taught in stages.

First: Man was taught that there was a Supreme

Being, Infinite and All Powerful. That it was the Creator who created all things above and below. That man was created by this Almighty Being and having been created by Him, was his son—that this Almighty was man's Heavenly Father.

Second: When man was created the Creator placed within the body of man a spirit or soul which never died but continued on through eternity.

Third: When man was created it was ordained that his material body should return to the earth from which it was taken. When this material body died it released the soul which went into the world beyond, there to wait until it was called upon to occupy another material body.

Apparently, as soon as his primitive mind could grasp the facts, he was taught that his soul was given a task. This task was for the soul to rule the material body by overcoming material desires. When this was accomplished his soul would be called back to the Great Source, and forever afterwards live in perfect joy and happiness.

He was taught that one material life was so short that the soul could not overcome all of the material desires, so it was ordained that his soul should come into many bodies until the task was accomplished; that these reincarnations were the salvation of his soul.

Fourth: It was thoroughly instilled into his mind that the Heavenly Father was *The Great Love* and that this great love ruled the Universe and never died.

He was taught that the love of the Heavenly Father was far greater than the love of his earthly father, who was only a reflection of his Heavenly Father. Therefore he should always approach his Heavenly Father without fear or dread and in perfect confidence and love, knowing that loving hands were being held out to receive him when he came.

Fifth: He was taught that all mankind were created by the same Heavenly Father; therefore all mankind were his brothers and sisters, and should be treated as such in all his dealings with them.

Sixth: Finally he was taught his duties on earth, how he should live to prepare himself to become fit to pass into the world beyond when he was called. He was especially reminded that he must follow the paths of Truth, Love, Charity, Chastity, with perfect love and confidence in his Heavenly Father.

From this short and inadequate sketch it is shown that the fundamental principles of the first religion of man were: *The Fatherhood of God and the Brotherhood of Man.*

Judging from the various religious teachings of the Sacred Inspired Writings, the phrase "Brotherhood of Man" is not meant to convey the idea that all men are to look upon each other as blood brothers. It would seem to me that this phrasing is symbolical or used as an example for explanation. I think our modern example better explains the meaning to the mind of present man, namely, "Do unto others as you would have them do unto you." This seems to be confirmed by the forty-two questions in the Osirian Ritual. If we all followed this "Golden Rule" no discord could arise among mankind and the world would be in a virtual bond of brotherhood.

Again, I think the meaning of the word "charity" is not fully comprehended today. It refers to the soul rather than to the material part of man. Not only material charitable actions, such as feeding the hungry and clothing the naked, but it includes good and charitable thoughts of others. We should think ill of no one but try to help them overcome their failings. The great Master, Jesus, gave us an example of this.

SYMBOLS.—Throughout his teachings early man was constantly reminded that no symbol, however sacred, was to be worshipped in any way; that symbols were used only to enable him to concentrate his mind solely on the Deity and the particular subject of his supplication. By keeping his eyes on the symbol, other objects were excluded from his vision.

Symbols in our churches would not be amiss today, at least in some cases. On one occasion my seat in church was directly behind the pew of a wealthy broker. Every time the congregation knelt in prayer this pillar of the church, for he was one of them, drew from the shelf a book bound as a prayer book. When he opened it I saw that it was a ledger with rows of figures in debit and credit columns. These he went up and down with his finger, all the time mumbling something so that those around him thought he was earnest in prayer. Were his thoughts of God? The symbol he was using guided him to the material—not the spiritual.

THEOLOGY.—The religion of Mu had no theologies or dogmas. Everything was taught in the simplest, most comprehensive language, a language that even the most unschooled mind could grasp.

Theologies and dogmas crept into religion after the submergence of the Motherland. With her destruction, her controlling influences were gone. Confusions in religion then began, and exist in full force today. Anyone considering present-day religion can see that it is in the process of crumbling, that it is only a question of time when it will be a mass of ruins. Then, when these ruins are cleared away, there will arise a new and purer conception of spiritual things. Religion cannot die until man has attained the perfection ordained for him.

Our present religious state is not a new condition. Twice before, religion has fallen to the ground through theologies and their consequences. Out of the ashes new religions have arisen. Out of the ashes of present religions a new one will also arise. "He whom the gods destroy they first make mad." Madness in the form of bigotry, impossible theologies, and other errors exists today.

WHY PAST RELIGIONS HAVE FALLEN.—At various times in the history of man unscrupulous priesthoods have caused the downfall of religion by introducing into it vicious systems of theology made up of inventions, extravagances and immorality; omissions and false and vicious translations from the Sacred Inspired Religion of Mu from which all religions have sprung.

These systems were invented by priesthoods for the purpose of inspiring superstitious fears in the hearts of the people, to ensnare them, body and soul, into slavery to the priesthood. Having accomplished this, it did not take long for these priesthoods to acquire wealth and become all powerful. This was vividly illustrated in Egypt, where the Priests of Ammon not only gained the riches of the country but seized the throne as well. When, however, they started to control the military, the soldiers revolted and at the point of the spear drove them down into Ethopia, where they were prevented from returning to Egypt. The accumulation and concentration of wealth invariably ruins a country. There are at least a dozen historical records of it.

The first great outrage to religion I have found historically recorded occurred in Atlantis 22,000 years ago. It is referred to as "extravagances in the priestly teachings." The great master, Osiris, dispelled these extravagances and reinstated the original religion of the Fatherhood of God and Brotherhood of Man. As a monument to the memory of this great master, Religion was named after him.

THE OSIRIAN RELIGION.—When Thoth of Atlantis founded the colony on the Nile Delta, Egypt's history began. Thoth built the first temple at Saïs and there taught Religion as purged by Osiris 6,000 years before.

33

THE SACRED SYMBOLS OF MU

At the destruction of Mu, Ra Mu, the King and High Priest of the Motherland, addressed the pleading crowds, saying:

"You shall all die together, you and your servants and your riches. From your ashes new nations shall arise and if they forget they are superior, not because of what they put on but what they put out, the same will befall them."

The foregoing indicates that the people had strayed from the teachings of the church, become materialistic and forgotten God, not that they had been led astray by the priests. It would appear that they were dropping the spiritual for the material: they were amassing riches and forgetting God. This would seem to be corroborated in a previous statement, where Ra Mu is quoted as saying:

"Did I not predict all this?"

It was the priesthood of Egypt that caused the cataclysmic wave of false gods, idolatry and spiritual degredation to sweep over the land. So well did they effect their nefarious designs that priestly orders throughout the world were drawn into the vortex contributing to religion's spiritual downfall. This started over 5,000 years ago, and the prostituted Osirian religion has now long passed into the discard. Many of its extravagances have, however, persisted down to present times and are found embodied in our religious conceptions.

The Egyptians were the first to teach the worship of symbols, a thing strictly forbidden in the Ancient Religion. Thus began idolatry. The next step was the invention of a devil whom they called Set. For this malevolent being they imagined a domain which they called Hell.

The extravagances of their description of this domain had no bounds, and one wonders how any sane person could have accepted them. According to these teachings, it was a place of everlasting flames, of burning brimstone that never died. Cast into these sulphurous flames, the Soul remained scorching for all eternity.

The soul of man is a spirit. No element can touch or come in contact with a spirit. Sulphur is an element. Therefore, it cannot come in contact with a spirit, for a spirit is negative to all elementary matter. Even if it were not, the forces of the spirit are so much higher than those of heat that the spirit could repel it.

I shall next show how the devil himself managed to put in an appearance. The claim was made that the devil was an archangel, fallen from the ways of grace, and cast from heaven into hell. The four archangels are only another vestment for the Four Great Primary Forces, or as Max Müller calls it, "a new disguise." As the Great Primary Forces still exist, working and controlling the Universe as of old, it is clear that none have fallen, as the story of Lucifer would have us believe.

It was thus the Egyptian priesthood dragged the beautiful pure Osirian Religion into the mud, the religion with which Egypt commenced her history 10,000 years before, causing the nation itself to fall and become the slave of foreign conquerors. Before the Egyptian invention, a devil was unknown. Man had been taught there were two influences attending him here on earth—a material influence emanating from his earthly body, and a spiritual influence that came from his soul. His spiritual influence had the power to overcome the material, and it was his destiny that it should eventually dominate. It might, however, take many incarnations before this was accomplished, after which his soul would return to the Great Source.

Hindu priests, always quick to adopt anything of material advantage to themselves, followed Egypt in the debauchery of religion. An obstacle that had first to be overcome, however, was their Naacal teachers. These were unwavering in their adherence to the teachings of the First Religion. So the Brahminical priests started to persecute the Naacals, eventually driving them into the snow-capped mountains of the North. When these holy men were disposed of, the debauch commenced.

Not wishing to borrow their devil from the Egyptians, the Brahmin priests invented one of their own and called him Siva (pronounced Sheva).

From the time Siva was grafted into the Hindu religion, history shows that the Hindus fell from the high pinnacle of civilization which had been theirs since the period of the Motherland. A little history will verify this assertion:

Universal History and M. D. Voltaire—A. D. 1758. Vol. 3, Page 13.

"The school of the ancient gynosophists was still subsisting in the great city of Benares on the banks of the Ganges. There the Brahmins cultivated the *Sacred Language* which they called *Hanferit,* and look upon it as the most ancient of all languages. [The Naacal writings are in what is here called Hanferit.]

"They admit of Genii, like the primitive Persians. They *tell* their *disciples* that symbols are made only to fix the attention of the people and are different *emblems* of the Deity. But as this sound theology *would turn to no profit,* they concealed it from the people. [And taught what produced superstitious awe and fear.]

"Be that as it may, the *Indians were no longer* that people of *superior knowledge* into whose country *the ancient Greeks used to travel for instruction."*

India was the cradle of the Greek Philosophy. Up to 500 B. C. the Greeks were going to India for learning. When they commenced going I do not know—possibly a thousand years before.

W. Robertson, "An Historical Disquisition of India," Pub. 1794, Page 274.

"The Brahmins, it is well known, *borrowed* religion, *as well as all other sciences* of civilization, *from the highly civilized Nagas,* whom afterwards they *relentlessly persecuted."*

One of the inventions of the Hindu priests was that Man was first created a grass, then a fish, passed into an amphibian, then a reptile, from a reptile into a mammal, and from this became a man. They also maintained that everything is a part of God and that all things put together are God. And yet this same priesthood says that idolatry is a sin. Let us analyze this.

Idolatry is a sin. The worship of idols made of wood and stone is idolatry. The worship of God is not idolatry. As the wood and stone are parts of God, the worship of wood and stone would be worshipping parts of God: therefore there is no such thing as idolatry, since whatever is worshipped is a part of God. What can be more fantastic than this? Yet I find the same conception in one of our religious sects today, and they call themselves Christians. Did Jesus ever utter such inconceivable nonsense?

The Brahminical priests did their work well, for they enslaved the people and froze their brains. *But—* India is today awakening. She is casting off her priestly shackles and has started to regain her enviable place among nations, to regain her old religion and civilization. And she will again stand in the proud position from which she was dragged down. The Untouchables will no longer be Untouchables, but will receive their place as brothers in the land. But the Hindus must remember that they are *only emerging,* the top of the Cross is not clear of the water.

Some few thousand years ago the Priesthoods generally put the coping stone of horrors on religion—they instituted the horrible practice of human sacrifice. This addition caused consternation and enhanced the fear of the people in all lands. No one knew but he might be the next to be stretched upon the bloody stone, or be shrouded in the flames of the fiery furnace. Fear and dread reigned supreme. These human sacrifices have supposedly disappeared from what is termed "civilized peoples." But have they? Is not human life sacrificed today under another guise? And what about present-day religions and people? The only difference from now and 3,000 years ago is a thicker veneer over our savagery.

The Church of Rome has a bloody page disfiguring its record by the Inquisition.

The Protestant Church has a great blot on her escutcheon with the burning of witches.

The Mohammedan Church was born with the sword, has lived by the sword, and will die by the sword—blood covers every page of its history.

Have Christians been following the teachings of the Great Master, Jesus, who preached only kindness and brotherly love? Certainly not! They have been following the cruel lust for blood bred of fanaticism and bigotry. Are we, ourselves, any better today? I think not. Our lust for blood causes us to hang, shoot and electrocute in the name of the law. What law? Not God's, for His law says, *"Thou shalt not kill."* With all our great professions of civilization we still remain savages at heart, and I have known many savages who are more truly civilized than we are. We erect towering buildings, make horrible wars on one another because of greed for power and wealth. Is this civilization, or mere display? Coat a pig with gold and the pig still remains a pig. The gold is only a veneer; the pig still exists in its original form. Our civilization is simply a veneer hiding our real selves—neither our hearts nor characters are affected by it for we are what we are.

I shall now show by Mu's Cosmogonic Diagram what the First Religion of Man was—the Sacred Inspired Religion of Mu.

Mu's Cosmogonic Diagram.—The Cosmogonic Diagram of Mu was the mother of all the various cosmogonic diagrams found throughout the world. All subsequent diagrams were based on that of the Motherland.

Inventions, alterations, additions in lines to adapt them to new meanings, made nightmares of them all.

One of the most prominent additions in the Hindu, Babylonian, Assyrian, Chaldean and Egyptian was the addition of a hell. This hell is shown in various diagrams as a small circle below the main figure, the outside of the circle symbolizing the Universe, which was putting it far away from the earth. As the devil was unknown in Mu, no hell appears in her cosmogonic diagram.

Deciphering Mu's Diagram.—In Mu the novice was taught to learn the diagram thoroughly and repeat what was written upon it as his spiritual convictions. Just as children are taught the Bible today, the children of lost Mu were instructed in this diagram.

The Construction of the Diagram.—In the cen-

Mu's Cosmogonic Diagram

ter is a circle within two crossed and interwoven triangles. Being interwoven or interlaced, these triangles form but one figure.

These two triangles are enclosed within a second circle, thus leaving twelve divisions.

Beyond this circle is a third, leaving a space between the two.

On the outside of this third circle are 12 scallops. Falling from the outside of the scallops is a ribbon which has 8 divisions.

THE MEANINGS OF THESE FIGURES.—The central circle is a picture of the Sun and the symbol of the Deity whose abode is Heaven.

The twelve divisions, formed by the crossing of the two triangles, are the gates to Heaven where dwells the Heavenly Father. These gates symbolize virtues, the twelve great earthly virtues, which man must possess before he can enter the gates, among them being Love, Hope, Charity, Chastity, Faith, et cetera. Love stands at the head of the list.

The space between the second and third circles is the world beyond, which the soul must pass through to reach the gates of Heaven.

The twelve scallops on the outside of the outer circle are the gates to the world beyond and symbolize the twelve great earthly temptations which must be overcome by the material body, before the soul can pass through these gates to the world beyond.

The ribbon with the eight divisions symbolizes the

The Babylonian Cosmogonic Diagram

eight roads to Heaven and tells what man's actions and thoughts must be to ascend to the gates of the world beyond. Put into present language the foregoing would read:

THE BELIEF.—I believe there are eight roads to travel to reach Heaven (mentioning them). My soul will first arrive after travelling these roads at the gates to the world beyond. To enter these my soul must show that my earthly body overcame the twelve great earthly temptations (mentioning them). Having shown that it had done so, my soul will be allowed to pass into the world beyond. This I must traverse until I reach the gates of Heaven. Here my soul must prove that my earthly body possessed the twelve great virtues (mentioning them). Having shown that it did, my soul will then be passed through the gates into Heaven to the Throne of Glory, where sits the Heavenly Father waiting to receive it.

Have we anything today in any of our religions and religious sects that will compare with this beautiful conception so simply worded?

This was the Religion of Mu, the Motherland, and the First Religion of Man.

JESUS AND THE CHRISTIAN RELIGION.—Jesus was a Master, the greatest and most proficient who has ever been on earth.

Jesus did not teach a new religion; he simply taught the First Original Religion as it is written in the Sacred and Inspired Writings of Mu.

The Chaldean Cosmogonic Diagram
The Sri Santara

The Lord's Prayer, the greatest work of its kind ever penned or spoken, is to be found in the Sacred Writings of Mu. Jesus condensed the ancient text to suit the language of his day. He compacted the whole of the material parts of religion into a few short sentences, leaving out nothing that was vital to man's salvation. The religion taught by Jesus has been called the Christian Religion, yet not five per cent of those who profess to follow His teachings do so; the other ninety-five per cent are following the supposed teachings of the apostles made up by a conclave of priests years after Jesus and his apostles had taken the long journey. This they called the Athenasian Creed. They borrowed the name Christian for their headline.

The teachings of this religion today include some of the extravagances the priesthood of Egypt grafted into the Osirian Religion, which are so contrary to actual teachings of Jesus they are deplorable. Theologies and bigotry, to which may be added supreme obstinacy, are tolling the death knell of the Christian religion. The priesthoods of this religion condemn the falling away of the world from the churches. This is easily understood by anyone who will trouble to think. But thinking priesthoods seem never to have existed. While they are bitterly complaining of this "falling away from the church," as they call it, the priesthood has only itself to blame. The public is receiving a higher education than heretofore. People are beginning to think for them-

The Hindu Cosmogonic Diagram

selves. Thinking shows them the impossible theories and beliefs that are being handed out to them, and the bigotry attending it all. With higher education their reasoning powers will not allow them to accept it, so they simply keep away from it.

Are people becoming irreligious? No! On the contrary, they are becoming more religious. The heart craves truth, a knowledge of the Loving Heavenly Father. Offer people a plain, untrammelled service of simplicity and truth and no church will be big enough to hold all those who will attend.

There is, however, a crisis in the Church today. How long before the structure will fall? It is crumbling fast and soon will form a heap of ruins on the ground.

With the atmosphere cleared, the Original Religion will return—the religion that places the spiritual above the material, that teaches the Love of the Heavenly Father, and makes a true brotherhood of man, as it did during the life of the Motherland.

I have stated that we still retain in our present religions some of the inventions and extravagances grafted into religion by the unscrupulous priesthood. They still persist, they have never been cleansed from our present day religions. I shall mention some; to mention all would fill volumes.

THE DEVIL AND HELL.—The origin and date already given.

VIRGIN BIRTH.—The origin of this is to be found in

the Sacred Writings of Mu. It appears in the Fifth Command of The Creation:

"From these cosmic eggs life came forth as commanded."

In a subsequent table explaining the commands in creation, cosmic eggs are referred to as "the virgins of Life." The sentence reads: "Hol Hu Kal." Translated into English it reads: Hol—closed; Hu—virgin womb; and Kal—to open. Free reading: To pierce or open the virgin womb; and, by permissible extension: To pierce or open the virgin womb of life.

For this reason the ancients called the waters "the mother of life"; for up to this period of the earth's history, no life had appeared. Life, therefore, first appeared in the waters. The advent of life had opened the virgin womb in the waters.

Later, The Four Great Creative Forces which emanate from the Deity had the additional name of Gods bestowed upon them.

Being the *First Known* commands or executors of the commands of the Creator, they were called of virgin birth to correspond with the teachings of the Sacred Writings regarding earthly life—thus the *First* life either of the Gods or nature was the result of Hol Hu Kal.

Upon this ancient conception modern priesthoods (within the last two thousand years) have invented virgin births and immaculate conceptions for various men that have lived, as an example, Masters. The Priest-hoods have made the Great Master, Jesus, of virgin birth and, forgetting themselves, give his pedigree and family tree back to David.

Our learned scholars are not to be surpassed by any priesthoods. They tell us that all ancient Kings were of virgin birth because they were "Sons of the Sun." These Kings claimed nothing of the kind. "Son of the Sun" was a title bestowed on the rulers or emperors of a colonial empire by Mu, the Empire of the Sun and Suzerain of the whole world.

Heretofore I have stated that Jesus did not teach a new faith but the Original Religion of Man.

My old friend, the Rishi, never tired of talking of the Great Master, Jesus. One day he said to me: "The Lord's Prayer, as the Christians call it, is the greatest masterpiece of phraseology and condensation ever written, for it embodies the whole of the ancient religion in a few short paragraphs. Take, for instance, the beginning, 'Our Father which art in Heaven.' In these six words many points in the ancient religion are covered. It first tells us that we are His children; therefore all mankind are brothers and sisters. "Forgive us our trespasses as we forgive others that trespass against us." These simple words tell us our duty one to the other, and that we should love one another like brothers and sisters. Again 'Our Father' tells us that we should approach Him as we would our earthly father, with love and confidence. "Give us this day our daily bread" is another wonderful sentence and far-reaching. It tells us that we should avoid greed and the craving to amass wealth and depend on Him for our daily needs. He will care for us, thus leaving us free to amass spiritual wealth without anxiety about the material.

"You will notice, my son, our temple has no wealth nor have those connected with it any wealth. We depend entirely on what the Heavenly Father sends us day by day through the people. Our faith in Him is implicit, so he never allows us to want." And so he could go on through every sentence of the Lord's Prayer.

Another favorite sentence in the Lord's Prayer to comment on was: *"Lead us not into temptation."* This, he said, "was unquestionably a mistranslation of the Master's words and, no doubt, was unintentional, arising from careless reading." He then went on: "Let us reason it out. In one of the paragraphs it is shown that the Heavenly Father is the *All Powerful,* for it says: 'For Thine is the Kingdom, the *Power* and the Glory.' Here it is shown that the supposed leader into temptation is the All Powerful. Therefore, being All Powerful, He cannot fail; and who is the All Powerful? Our kindly Heavenly Father whose love is so great it rules the universe. Could He forget His great love and set a trap for a son's downfall? Impossible!

"I think the words of the Master, correctly translated, would be: *'Let* us not be led into temptation'; for in the Sacred Writings we find: 'O Heavenly Father, let not temptation overtake or surround us. If it does, deliver us from it.' These are the reasons why I feel that the words of the Great Master have been unintentionally misquoted or mistranslated."

He told me that one of the cardinal themes of the Great Master, Jesus, was re-incarnation, something almost entirely omitted in our Biblical account of Him, also in our religious services.

He told me many legends about Jesus that permeated Oriental lore, one of which he said was universal and told everywhere. The scene is laid in Lahore where Jesus was staying with one, Ajainin, who was one of Jesus' pupils.

One day Jesus and Ajainin were sitting in the porch of the temple and while sitting there a band of wandering minstrels entered the court and began to play. Their music was very rich and delicate, and Jesus remarked:

"Among the highest of the land we have no sweeter music than that which these uncouth children of the jungles bring to us."

Ajainin asked: "Whence do they get this talent? In one short life they surely could not acquire such perfection of voice and such knowledge of harmony and time."

Jesus answered: "Men call them prodigies. They are no prodigies; all things result from natural laws. These people are not young; a thousand years would not suffice to give them such divine expressions and such purity of voice. Ten thousand years ago these people had mastered harmony. In days of old they trod the busy thoroughfares of life and caught the melody of the voices of nature. They have come again to learn still other lessons from the varied notes of nature."

When walking one evening with the Rishi, talking on the subject of the many religions of today and the work of Christian missionaries, he related a tale that was popular among the native priesthood about a poor benighted Hindu and a Christian missionary.

"A missionary asked one of his native flock what he thought of religion having so many sects? The poor Hindu answered: Religions are like the fingers on the hand. How are we to tell which is right? There was once a dispute among the fingers of the hand as to which was entitled to preëminence.

"The thumb said, I ought to have the preëminence for it is plain none of you can do anything without me.

"Ah! said the first finger, What is more important than pointing out the way? This is my office. I ought to have the preëminence.

"I, said the second finger, rest my claims on mathematical principles. When you hold the hand upright which finger is the tallest? I am; therefore I ought to have the preëminence.

"No, said the third finger, for although it is something to point out the way, and mathematics are strong, there is one thing stronger, and that is love. When you put the symbol of love upon the hand, it is on the third finger. Therefore the supremacy is mine.

"Hear me, too, said the little finger, it is true I

am small and you are large. Mathematics are strong and love is stronger. But there is one thing above all these and that is worship. When you approach God, I am the finger you choose to present nearest in your prayers. For then you press your hands together, lift them up and hold them thus. Therefore, I should have the preëminence."

And the old Rishi turned to me with a smile, saying: "What is your comment, my son?" The poor, benighted Hindu's philosophy nonplussed me. So I leave it to my readers to supply it.

On one occasion the old Rishi informed me that temple legends stated: "Jesus, during his sojourn in the Himalayan monastery, studied the contents of the Sacred Inspired Writings, the language, the writing and the Cosmic Forces of the Motherland."

That Jesus was a Master of the Cosmic Forces, with a perfect knowledge of the Original Religion, is manifest in the Books of the New Testament; but it is not there shown that he understood the language of Mu. His acquaintance with it is proved by his last words when nailed to the Cross: *"Eli, Eli, lama sabac tha ni."*

This is not Hebrew nor any tongue that was spoken in Asia Minor during the life of Jesus. It is the pure tongue of the Motherland, badly pronounced and spelt in the New Testament. It should have been spelt, read and pronounced: *"Hele, hele, lamat zabac ta ni."*

Translation:

Hele—I faint. *Hele*—I faint; *lamat zabac ta ni*—darkness is coming over my face.

I do not stand alone on this translation. The late Don Antonio Batres Jaurequi, a prominent Maya scholar of Guatemala, in his book, "History of Central America," says: "The last words of Jesus on the Cross were in Maya, the oldest known language." He says they should read, "Hele, Hele, lamah sabac ta ni." Put in English: "Now I am fainting; the darkness covers my face." Thus we virtually agree on all material points. The slight differences are easily explained.

Jaurequi spells the word "lama*h*." I spell it "lama*t*." He spells the word "*s*abac." I spell it "*z*abac." This difference is brought about by the translations coming from two different lines of colonization. Mine comes from the Naga-Maya of Eastern Asia; Jaurequi's comes from the modern Maya of Central America. The two, taken from vastly distant parts of the earth, agree in all material points.

CHAPTER III

SYMBOLS OF THE DEITY AND HIS ATTRIBUTES

SACRED SYMBOLS.—To make the Sacred Symbols as intelligible as possible to my readers I am dividing them into classes. I shall start with the highest, most Sacred Symbol of all, the Sun as Ra symbolizing the Deity. It is the collective symbol representing the Deity with all His attributes, and the only symbol that does so.

Next will be given symbols of His various attributes. Although I have narrated the Tale of the Creation in my first book, *The Lost Continent of Mu,* I am repeating it in this one for two reasons. First:— All symbols connected with the Creation were looked upon as sacred, and were used in religious ceremonies. Second:— In the version I am now giving I am extending it slightly, which makes it come nearer to the original version.

This will be followed by symbols used in religious teaching.

The following chapter will be the compound Sacred Symbols, with the changes from their beginnings.

Decipherings of all symbols are given either accompanying the symbol or in "The Lost Continent of Mu."

This being the third book of a trilogy on Mu, I have not repeated in it various decipherings, but have referred to "The Lost Continent," where they will be found.

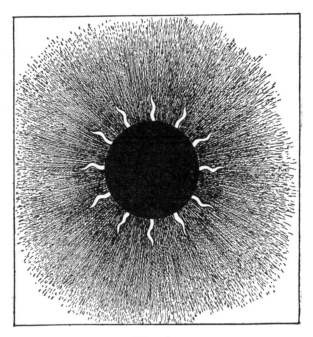

The Sun

SYMBOLS OF THE DEITY.—*The Sun* was the *Monotheistic Symbol* of the *Deity*. As the monotheistic or collective symbol it was called RA, and being the *monotheistic* symbol it was looked upon as the most Sacred of all the Sacred Symbols.

While each attribute of the Deity, in several cases, had various symbols expressing it, there was only *one* monotheistic or collective symbol.

During the early history of man there were no gods but the *One Great Infinite*. The gods crept into religious ceremonies later. The beginning of the gods was when the Four Great Creative Forces were given the name of gods.

Scientists and archaeologists, not comprehending the ancient form of writing and symbolisms, have unfortunately spread broadcast the error that the ancients worshipped the Sun, when the fact is that they regarded the Sun *as a symbol only;* and when they dedicated a temple to the Sun, *it was to the Almighty* as either the Deity, the One Lord God, or to the Almighty as His male attribute in creation.

The Attributes of the Deity

The Creator's Two Principles.—This is one of the most interesting of the ancient conceptions. It arose from the assumption that to produce anything, male and female were required; so that gave the Creator the two principles—the sun symbolizing the male and the moon the female.

Symbols were then designed to express the different phases, if it can be so called. First a symbol was devised to express the dual capacity; this they called *Lahun* ⊕ the English translation of which being "two in one, one in two" and by extension "all in one and one is all." The glyph Lahun is a circle with a bar drawn through its center. The Mexican Tablet No. 150 shows the Sun symbolizing the male principle and the same cut shows the moon symbolizing the female principle.

It was quite usual among the ancients, when erecting temples, to build two near each other. The larger one was dedicated to the Sun as the male principle and the

No. 150

smaller to the Moon as the female. The lines on Tablet No. 150 read: "The Creator created one. One became two and two produced three from whom all mankind descended." The top face symbolizes the Sun; the lower face without rays the moon.

Isis: The Egyptians were not content with having the Moon symbolize the female attribute of the Creator, so they devised a symbol for the moon which they called Isis; thus they made a symbol to symbolize a symbol.

59

The intricacies of what Isis was, beyond symbolizing Nature, and being the executrix of God's commands, was only understood by the Egyptians themselves, and they were not all in accord on the subject.

In ceremonies and processions Isis wore as her headdress a moon with a pair of cow's horns. With the Egyptians, cow's horns symbolized motherhood. The goddess Sati of Upper Egypt, and the goddess Hathor both had cow's horns in their headdress. Hathor had a

Isis

moon also like Isis. It appears to me that Sati, Hathor and Isis all symbolized the same thing, only they were represented in slightly different vestments.

The old Oriental Empires followed the Egyptians in making a woman symbolize the moon.

The Babylonians had Astoreth. The Hittites had

Hepet. The Greeks rejoiced in their Aphrodite, and the Romans in Venus.

Papyrus Ani: "In early days, before priests froze the thoughts of man into blocks of stone and built of them shrines to a thousand gods, many held that there was only One God."

THE DEITY AS THE CREATOR.—The Creation was one of the principal themes of the Ancients. In this they clearly distinguished between the Creator Himself and the work consummated, making a prominent dividing line in their symbols. I shall first take the symbols of the Deity as the Creator. The ancients looked upon the power of Creation as one of the attributes of the Almighty.

The ancients had numerous figures, always conventional, symbolizing this attribute. Apparently the most popular were adorned serpents. Many designs of these serpents are found in ancient carvings and literature.

Two of these serpents are especially prominent. One was the cobra, called in the Motherland, Naga. This one had *seven* heads. This number was given to correspond with the seven stages of creation, the seven mental planes, et cetera.

The seven-headed serpent originated in Mu and was there called *Naga*. In various Mu colonies it received added names. Judging from the geographical position of the colonies where we find it, I think that the lower western half of Mu was where it was used. The people using this symbol were called after it—the Nagas.

Angkor Thom

Anarajapoora—Ceylon

The other serpent was covered with feathers instead of scales. This also originated in the Motherland and was there called *Quetzacoatl*. It is still to be found in the impenetrable jungles and swamps of Yucatan and Central America, but extremely rare. During all of my explorations I have only seen one, and I never want to see another. It is the most venomous serpent ever known on earth. Its location was apparently along the northern half of the Motherland. One tribe who made Quetzacoatl their symbol for the Creator, like the Nagas took their name from it, being known as—the Quetzals. The Quetzacoatl varied in design among these people.

One of the most noteworthy conventional designs of the Quetzacoatl is the *Dragon* so prominent in the northern parts of eastern Asia today. In this effort the ancients carried the design to the extreme of conventionality, for they endowed it with a crest, which it had not, wings which it had and legs which were long instead of mere claws or feet. They not only gave it the wherewithal to fly, but to run also, which it could not do.

The Pueblo Indians of Arizona and New Mexico bestowed on it the name of the bearded serpent as well as Quetzacoatl.

The Quiche Mayas, in their sacred book the Popal Vuh, refer to it as follows:—

"All was immobility and silence in the darkness, in the night; only the Creator, the maker, the dominator, *the Serpent covered with feathers,* they who engender,

Narayana

they who create, they are surrounded by green and blue, their name is Gucumatz."

The name Gucumatz here does not refer to the Creator Himself but to His Four Great Creative Forces, hence they are referred to as "they."

I found in a Nootka Indian tableau a serpent having a plume on his head, unquestionably one of the conventional designs of Quetzacoatl. Although the names of all other objects in the tableau were given, that of the Serpent was omitted by these British Colombian Indians.

As *Sacred Symbols of the Creative Powers,* these were all held in great reverence. They stood next to the Sun—the most sacred symbol of all.

I also find a feathered serpent in Egypt. In the tomb of Pharaoh Seti I is to be seen a painting of a serpent having three heads, four legs of man and *feathered wings.*

THE SACRED FOUR.—The Sacred Four is among the oldest religious conceptions. I found it in the Sacred Inspired Writings of Mu.

The Sacred Four are the Four Great Primary Forces,

coming from the Almighty. They first brought order out of chaos throughout the Universe and then, on command, created the Universe with all the bodies and life therein. When creation was completed they were given charge of the physical universe. Today the Universe and all physical life is controlled by these Forces.

An ancient Hindu picture

The god Vishnu supported by the Serpent Ananta, having seven heads, the symbol of the Seven Commands of Creation.

The ancients held these Forces in such reverence that nearly if not all of the very early temples were dedicated to them as the Creator's executors. Most of the temples, I find, were subsequently dedicated to the Sun and Moon, the Sun Temple symbolizing the male principle of the Creator and the Temple of the Moon the female principle. Still later, I find temples dedicated

66

to Seven Great Commands of Creation and symbolized by an adorned or conventional Serpent.

From the beginning various symbols for the Sacred Four began to creep in. Also a plurality of names were given them at different times by various people. I have a collection of over fifty names given to them. Among them are: the Four Great Ones, the Four Powerful Ones, the Four Great Kings, the Four Great Maharajas, the Four Great Builders, the Four Great Architects, the Four Great Geometricians, the Four Great Pillars; and today we call them the Four Archangels.

Somewhere about 6,000 or 7,000 years ago, a confusion was caused by giving the Pillars *Keepers,* which were called Genii. This addition of keepers for the Pillars must have occurred after the destruction of Mu, as I do not find them in any writings of the First Civilization. The Pillars were placed at the Four Corners of the earth to teach ancient man the Four Cardinal points. The earth's symbol is a four-sided square, which when referring to anything but the Cardinal points is shown with sides, top and bottom parallel, thus ▢ and when associated with the Cardinal points or referring to them is placed thus ◇ so that the points shall be in their true position. The crossing of these two squares was used by the Egyptians to symbolize the eight Roads to Heaven. ✧

The writings about the Genii are so obtuse and so mixed up that I cannot look upon them as anything but a camouflage for the Pillars, consequently the changing of the name from the Sacred Four to Genii is a change of vestment only.

BIRDS SYMBOLS OF THE SACRED FOUR.—Birds as symbols play an important part in the ancient religious conceptions but what they actually symbolized remained for the Mexican Tablets to tell us. We have an Egyptian record in their ancient god Seb, but what is said about him by the Egyptians is so purely symbolical, that without other evidences, the layman could hardly be brought to understand (see Plate II).

THE GOD SEB: *Egyptian Book of the Dead.* Here the god Seb is called "the Father of the Gods," "the Bearer of the Gods" and "the Leader of the Gods." Seb was also called "the Great Cackler which produced the Mundane Egg." He is spoken of as having "laid the egg out of which the earth and all therein came forth." It further says: "I protect the egg of the Great Cackler, if I thrive it thrives, if I live it lives, if I breathe the breath of air it breathes." The god carries on his head the figure of a goose. Seb was the Egyptian name for this particular species of goose.

The foregoing speaks of both the Creator and the Four Great Creative Forces emanating from Him. As hitherto stated, "the Gods" were the Sacred Four, thus showing that the old Egyptians knew perfectly well what the Origin of Forces is.

Hawaiian Tradition: Ellis' Polynesian Research. "In the Sandwich Islands there is a tradition saying that in the beginning there was nothing but water when a big bird descended from on high and laid an egg in the sea. The egg burst and Hawaii came forth."

It was Mexico, however, that has given us the clinching proof of what bird symbols of the ancients really signified. Among Niven's collection of Mexican Tablets, there are over fifty showing birds. I have selected one to decipher, to tell what they all mean.

Mexican Tablet No. 1086: Those who have read my two books—*The Lost Continent of Mu* and *The Children of Mu* will readily see the meaning of two glyphs which I here point out in the bird figure.

The eye of the bird ⊚ is the Uighur form of the monotheistic symbol of the Deity.

Projecting from the bird's breast is the hieratic letter H in the alphabet of Mu ⊡ which was among all ancient people the alphabetical symbol for the Four Great Forces. The body of the bird is in the shape of a pod—symbol for the home of the primary forces. The various lines in connection with the pod are old esoteric Uighur temple writings.

This bird therefore symbolizes the Creative Forces of the Deity and the forces are shown as emanating from or coming out of the Deity. By extension, this figure reads: A symbol of the Almighty showing the four Great Primary Forces coming out of Him.

Easter Island: On this little island have been found various bird symbols and conventional animals with birds' heads. One has an egg in its claw, which seems to show that the ancient Easter Islanders had the same conceptions as the Hawaiians.

Legends of some of the North American Indians show that bird symbols are their favorite symbol for the Creative Forces. Their name for this bird is the Thunder Bird.

Birds appear among the ancient records of the Babylonians, Chaldeans and Hittites as one of their symbols of the Sacred Four—The Creative Forces.

The Assyrian Genii included a bird.

The Egyptians included a bird.

The Bible also includes a bird.

An Alaskan Totem Pole: A very old chief of the tribe

of Haiden Indians, Queen Charlotte Island, Alaska, to which a totem pole belongs has stated: "The winged creature which crowns the totem pole is the Thunder Bird and represents the Great Creator." It would have been more correct if he had said: "Represents the Great Creative *Forces*."

I am under the impression that the winged circle got its inspiration from a bird symbol. This ancient conception remains dear to us; for whenever heavenly beings are depicted, they are shown with wings like a bird.

All the various bird symbols, from so many widely diversified spots, express the same conception, and it seems to me that, different as they are in appearance, they must have a common ancestor.

CROSS SYMBOLS OF THE SACRED FOUR.—The Specialized Cross was one of the figures used by the ancients to denote the Sacred Four—the Four Great Primary Forces. The cross was always a favorite symbol among the ancients probably because they found it more expressive than any other figure. Studying and writing about the Sacred Four appears also to have been an absorbing theme with them. Today the Pueblo Indians of Arizona and New Mexico refer to the Sacred Four as "Those above."

The mother of all crosses was plain with four arms of equal length. I first find it in the Sacred and Inspired Writings as the symbol of The Sacred Four—The Great Creative Forces.

Mexican Tablet No. 672: Is an exact duplication of

71

the cross heretofore mentioned as appearing in the Oriental copies of the Sacred Inspired Writings of Mu. As time went on this cross evolved. It developed into

No. 672

four distinct lines, becoming more intricate all the time.

1. The end of the first line and the shortest, I have called the Pyramid Cross.

2. The end of the second line is a cross formed of four loops, having the symbol of the Deity in the center. These I have called the Loop Crosses.

3. The end of the third line is the well-known Swastika, known as "the good luck symbol."

4. The end of the fourth line was the winged circle. The ancients rioted in designs for this figure; the Egyptians excelling others in beautiful devices and marvelous artistry.

Besides these four main lines, there were many single special designs.

THE PYRAMID CROSS. LINE 1.—A group of Crosses among Niven's collection of Mexican tablets is especially interesting. I have called them the Pyramid Crosses because they are designed on the lines of a pyramid. They are the cosmogony of a pyramid illustrated by a cross.

The four arms are composed of four triangles corresponding with the four sides of a pyramid.

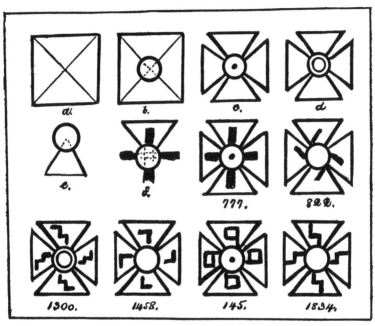

The points of these triangles are covered with the monotheistic symbol of the Deity.

The base of a pyramid is square; the four triangles brought together form a square. The pyramid is built on astronomical lines; so is the Cross.

These Crosses were drawn before the submersion of Mu. Were any pyramids built before that date? I know of none. Were pyramids evolved out of these Crosses?

Fig. A. Is the base of a pyramid divided into four triangles.

73

Fig. B. Dotted lines within the circle show the points of the triangles, corresponding to the top of a pyramid.

Fig. C. Shows the Cross with the monotheistic symbol of the Deity, Naga Pattern, crowning the points.

Fig. D. Is the same as Fig. C with the exception that the Uighur monotheistic symbol crowns the points.

Fig. E. The point of the triangle covered by the monotheistic symbol. The following is written on these tablets:

"The Four Great Pillars," "The Sacred Four," "The Four Great Architects," "The Four Great Builders" and "The Four Powerful Ones."

No. 777 confirms the fact that the four triangles forming the Cross are the Sacred Four because the symbol within the triangle reads: "Pillar." The four triangles with their inscriptions therefore read: "The Four Great Pillars"—one of the names given to the Sacred Four.

During the life of Mu it was taught that the Four Great Pillars sustained the Universe.

After the destruction of Mu the Universe was forgotten and the earth given the honor of anchoring and sustaining the Pillars. A pillar was placed at each of the Cardinal Points:—North, South, East and West.

THE LOOPED CROSSES. LINE 2.—The evolution of this line started with the plain cross shown in the Sacred Writings and ended with the Deity being added to four loops symbolizing the Four Great Forces, with the names of the Forces given within the loop.

The evolution of the Looped Crosses

Fig. 1. The Original Cross.

Fig. 2. The oldest form of Looped Cross I have as yet found. It is very ancient from the fact that the symbol of the Deity is of the ancient pattern and not specialized. It is a question in my mind whether a link is not missing between Fig. 1 and Fig. 2; the change appears to me to be too radical for the ancients.

Sometime during the teachings of primitive man trouble apparently began to accumulate over the circle, which was used to symbolize various things. It was then decided to specialize the circle which symbolized the Deity. The Nagas added a dot in the center and the Uighurs an inner circle. Fig. 2 has neither of these specializations.

Fig. 3ª. Is the same as Fig. 2 except that Fig. 3ª has the Naga pattern of the symbol for the Deity.

Fig. 3ᵇ. Is the same as Fig. 2 except that this cross has the Uighur pattern for the symbol of the Deity.

Fig. 4. This figure shows the last addition to the Looped Crosses. Within the arms of the loops the names of the Force are written, in this case the name of the

Force being "builder" ⌐ (a two-sided square). The

loop is a symbol that a certain divine order has been carried out. The Force has returned to the giver of the command.

A group of representative Looped Crosses taken from Niven's Mexican Tablets

Various other Crosses were used by the ancients in their writings, and each one had a different meaning. They are however easily distinguishable from the Crosses symbolizing the Sacred Four. The original Cross of the Sacred Four was a solid plain cross; all the others are open crosses.

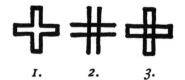

1. 2. 3.

1. This Cross reads *U-luumil* which means "the

76

Land of," "the Country of," "the Empire of," et cetera.

2. Another Cross is formed by four lines drawn across each other.

3. Sometimes but not often we find the ends of this Cross connected. The meaning of it is "slowly," "little by little," "slow progress," et cetera.

THE SWASTIKA. LINE 3.—The Swastika was originally associated with good luck from being the favorite symbol of the Sacred Four who were in charge of the physical Universe and therefore the means by which all good things came to man. While the Swastika is one of the oldest and most universal of symbols, being found throughout the ancient world, its origin and meaning have been lost for the past 3,500 years. The loss occurred when the fierce Brahminical priesthood of India persecuted and drove their teachers, the mild and highly educated Naacals, into the snow-capped mountains of the North.

I found the origin and meaning of this symbol:

First: In the Naacal writings which were brought from the Motherland and for thousands of years, probably, had lain dust covered and almost forgotten in the archives of Oriental temples and monasteries.

Second: Confirmed by the Mexican Stone Tablets.

Fate, however, ordained that their coverings of dust and ashes of thousands of years should be removed and their secrets be once more known to the world.

The "good luck symbol" is a very appropriate name for the Swastika, since it represents the physical welfare of man and all the Universe. The Swastika evolved from the plain original Cross.

1.   2.   3.   4.   5.

The Evolution of the Swastika:

Fig. 1. Is the orginal plain Cross.

Fig. 2. Here we have a circle added, surrounding the Cross. The Circle is the symbol of the Deity. The Cross is shown within the Deity; therefore it is a part of Him, emanating from Him. This accounts for the ancients calling their works: "the Commands of the Creator," "His Desires," "His Wishes," et cetera. The Forces symbolized by the Cross were the executors of His commands. With the circle drawn around the Cross it became a composite glyph symbolizing the ancient's full Godhead of Five—i. e. The Deity and His Four Great Primary Forces, the Four original Gods.

Fig. 3. Is a glyph found among the North American cliff writers. The arms of the Cross extend beyond the circle.

Fig. 4. The next step was to project the arms beyond the circle and turn their ends down at *right angles* ⌐ thus forming a two-sided square, which was the ancient glyph for "Builder." Thus were shown the Four Great Builders of the Universe. Without question it soon became evident to the ancients that by extending the original Cross they had deprived themselves of the possibility of mentioning the Four Great Forces without including the Deity. They could not write the Sacred Four, but they must write the full Godhead of five. To rectify this and bring back the symbol to its original meaning they eliminated the circle, leaving only the Four Great Builders of the Universe.

Throughout the world have been found glyphs which archaeologists have called Swastikas. I refer to a glyph which is formed by crossing the hieratic letters N ⟍ which are crossed thus ∝ This is not a Swastika but the diphthong *Sh* in the Motherland's alphabet. Where the ends of a cross are *curved,* it is not a Swastika. The arms of a Swastika must be bent over at *perfect right angles* to form a *perfect two-sided square,* the symbol for "Builder."

Clement of Alexandria wrote: "These Four Powerful Ones, these Four Canobs, these Heavenly Architects, emanate from the Great Supreme Infinite One, and evolved the material Universe from chaos."

1.) *2.* *3.* *4.*

THE WINGED CIRCLE. LINE 4.—Apparently there was only one step between the original cross and the winged circle, unless we accept the Mexican butterfly winged circle as a step.

Fig. 1. The Original Cross.

Fig. 2. Dhyan Choans. Ancient, Oriental, and Mexican.

Fig. 3. Butterfly winged Circle. Mexican.

Fig. 4. Bird winged Circle. Hindu.

As will be seen, in all cases except one, the circles have feathered wings. All these, I believe, originated since the destruction of Mu. The Butterfly winged circle was in existence before Mu went down. The winged circle was popularly received by all people but everyone appears to have had a different conception of how it should be designed. The Egyptian designs exceeded all others in gorgeously beautiful feather work.

TRUNCATED FIGURES.—Among the Mexican Tablets —Niven's collection—I find over one hundred peculiar truncated figures. They are purely conventional and were not intended to represent any of Nature's lives.

On deciphering them I found that they are symbolical of the workings of two of the Great Primary Forces.

The trunk indicates the direction in which these Forces work. The body is that of a chrysalis or pod, the symbol for the home of the Primary Forces. The lines are the numeral writings of the ancients—Uighur pattern.

The legs and arms point to the positions of these Forces under certain conditions.

Truncated Figures
From Niven's collection of Mexican prehistoric tablets

THE SACRED SYMBOLS OF MU

CHINESE SYMBOLS.—From the Chinese writings it is hard to tell whether Fig. 1 was the symbol for the

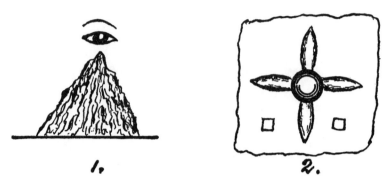

1.   *2.*

Sacred Four or the Four Genii or both. The mountain was called *Yo*. Fig. 2 is a jade ornament from Peking. It is one of the symbols of the Sacred Four, and looked upon as a sacred emblem by the Chinese.

THE SCARAB.—Hitherto the Scarab beetle has been looked upon as a symbol of Egyptian origin. I am here giving records which prove that the Scarab beetle was used as a symbol of creative energy in the Motherland tens of thousands of years before men settled in Egypt.

1.   *2.*   *3.*

Fig. 2. Is a little tableau carved on the handle of a knife. A record exists saying that this knife was worn by Prince Maya of India. Prince Maya was the son of the first ruler over the Naga Empire of India. Traditions say that Prince Maya lived 25,000 years ago; other traditions say 35,000 years ago. Temple histories show that the Naga Empire was in existence 25,000 years ago. Inscriptions on the handle of this knife state that it was made *before* India was turned into a Colonial Empire.

It is believed, based on a tradition, that this knife was made in the Motherland and obtained there by Prince Maya who brought it back to India on his return after he had completed his studies in a Naacal College. It is without question the oldest known knife in the world. When it was presented to me by an Indian prince, a written history was given with it, telling what ancient kings had worn it.

Referring back to the tableau, the Scarab is shown surrounded by rays of glory, and kneeling in adoration are two deer called *Ceh.* This species of deer was the ancient symbol for *first man. Ceh* is often shown as the symbol for first man in ancient writings, both Hindu and Maya. Upper Egypt was colonized from India. Without question, the colonists brought this symbol with them, so that the Scarab as a sacred symbol originated not in Egypt but in Mu the Motherland whence it was brought to Egypt by way of India.

Fig. 3. Is one of the vignettes of the Book of the Dead and is a reflex of the symbol just described.

Fig. 1. Is a vignette of the Egyptian god *Khepra* also taken from the Book of the Dead.

Egyptian writings vary somewhat as to what the scarabaeus beetle actually symbolizes.

The *name Khepra* is derived from the Egyptian word *kheper,* to create.

On the tablet of Ramases II at Kuban we read:—"The God Ra is like thee in his limbs, the god Khepra in creative Force."

From the writings of Anana, 1320 B. C.:—"To the Egyptians the Scarabaeus beetle is no god, but an emblem of the Creator, because it rolls a ball of mud between its feet and sets therein its eggs to hatch, as the Creator rolls the world around, thereby causing it to produce life."

GANESHA.—Ganesha is the symbol of the attribute who cares for the welfare of the crops and fields, and is generally known as "The Lord of the crops and fields" upon which humanity depends for its sustenance. On that account he is very much beloved.

Ganesha is depicted as having a man's body painted red with an elephant's head placed upon it.

In India he is to be found at the crossroads sitting upon a stone.

Dear old Ganesha, (for he is very old, having originated in the Motherland) everyone loves him, even the little children. No one ever passes him without placing a flower between his arms, so that he is always bedecked with flowers.

In Java he is more thought of still, for there he is held to be the emblem of good luck also, and his

84

Ganesha from India

Ganesha from Java

representation is found everywhere, over the doors of shops, on bank windows; in fact no place apparently can be lucky without him. The Javanese give him Four Arms corresponding with the Four Great Primary Forces from which we receive all our blessings.

CHAPTER IV

THE CREATION

VIGNETTES FROM THE SACRED WRITINGS OF MU.—

Fig. 1. Fine, straight, horizontal lines. Symbol for Space.

Fig. 2. Symbolizing the Seven-headed Serpent as the Deity moving through Space. The surrounding circle is the symbol for the Universe.

Fig. 3. Wavy horizonal lines symbolize Earthly Waters.

Fig. 4. The Circle. The monotheistic symbol of the Deity.

Fig. 5. The Plain Cross. Symbol of the Sacred Four. The Four Great Primary Forces coming direct from the Almighty.

Fig. 6. The full Godhead of Five. The Deity and his Four Great Primary and Creative Forces.

Fig. 7. Lahun. The dual principle of the Creator.

Fig. 8. The Fires of the Underneath. The Earth's Center.

Fig. 9. Vertical, fine, dotted lines from the Sun symbolize the Sun's affinitive Forces to the Earth's Light Forces.

Fig. 10. Vertical, fine, straight lines from the Sun, symbolize the Sun's affinitive Forces to the Earth's Light Forces.

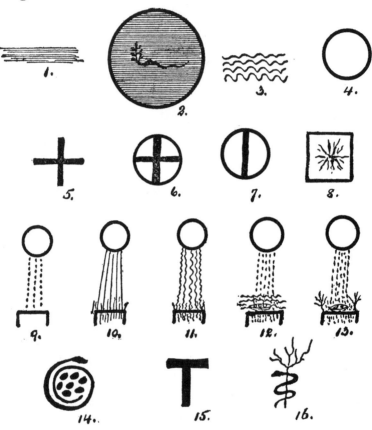

Fig. 11. Vertical, wavy lines from the Sun, symbolize the Sun's affinitive Force to the Earth's Heat Force.

Fig. 12. The Sun's affinitive Forces to the Earth's Life Forces striking the Earth's Forces in the Cosmic Eggs formed in the waters.

Fig. 13. The Sun's affinitive Forces to the Earth's

88

Life Forces striking the Earth's Forces in Cosmic Eggs which have been formed on the land.

Fig. 14. Symbol of the Waters as the Mother of Life.

Fig. 15. The Tau, symbol of Resurrection and Emersion.

Fig. 16. The Tree of Life and the Serpent. The Serpent symbolizes the Waters and the Tree—Mu, the Mother of Man, the Only Life. All of nature's lives are illusion; they do not continue on. Only man is Life and Life is everlasting.

Mexican Tablet No. 1231: I consider this cross the most valuable writing which has come down to us from the First Civilization both as regards religion and science. This cross tells us that all Forces throughout the Universe have their origin in the Deity. That these Forces are controlling life and all movements of matter down to the atom and particles of atoms, either directly or indirectly. It shows us that the Forces called Atomic Forces are only indirect workings of Primary Forces through Atoms. It tells us how the Great Primary Forces are working in a manner to maintain regular and perfect movements of each and every body throughout the Universe.

All of the arms of this cross are symbols of the Primary Forces coming from and out of the Deity. All of these arms or Forces are pointing towards the East —the four form a circle. Therefore, the Primary Forces are all working in a circle from a Center and proceed-

Tablet No. 1231

ing in an Easterly direction.

Detailed deciphering of this symbol is to be found in *The Lost Continent of Mu,* Page 34.

The Origin of Forces has always been a mooted question among scientists. We have here a writing by the scientists of the earth's First Great Civilization, telling us what the origin is; and not only that, but also the manner and direction of their workings. Especially it shows us the curvatures apparent throughout the Universe, which are causing so much controversy among scientists today.

N⁰ 988.

How long ago this was written I cannot say: but certainly more than 12,000 years ago.

Mexican Tablet No. 988: I am giving this tablet as

a confirmation of the previous one regarding the direction in which the Forces are working throughout the Universe. This particular glyph shows the lines running from the outside to the Center—therefore it is the Centripetal Force.

This glyph, without any script, appears on many of the Yucatan and Central American inscriptions.

Pedro Beltram, Le Plongeon and others have written that this glyph refers to the movement of the Sun. Here it distinctly states that it represents the workings of a primary Force.

N⁰·339.

Mexican Tablet No. 339: This interesting little tablet symbolizes the Four Great Primary Forces, in the shape of a butterfly, flying through space and evolving law and order out of chaos in obedience to the command of the Creator—His first command in Creation.

Nº 1267.

"Let Land Appear"
"And waters covered the face of the earth"

A full deciphering of this tablet is given in *The Lost Continent of Mu,* Page 37.

Mexican Tablet No. 1267:

Fig. 1. The outside circle—The Universe.

Fig. 2. The wavy circle—The Waters.

Fig. 3. The inside—The Earth.

Fig. 4. "The Fires of the underneath"—Volcanic gases. The Force symbol, coming out of the Fires, tells us that land is about to be raised.

Mexican Tablet No. 328: This Mexican tablet symbolizes the actual first life on earth. A full reading of this compound glyph is given in *The Children of Mu,* page 76.

THE TALE OF THE CREATION.—The following is what I found in the old Oriental Naacal writing, supplemented by the Mexican Tablets:

Naacal

"Originally the Universe was only a soul or spirit. Everything was without form and without life. All was calm, silent and soundless. Void and dark was the immensity of space. Only the Supreme Spirit, the Great Self-Existing Power, the Creator, the Seven-Headed Serpent, moved within the abyss of darkness."

"The desire came to Him to create worlds, and the

94

desire came to Him to create the earth with living
things upon it, and He created the earth and all therein.
This is the manner of the creation of the earth with all
there is within and upon it:—The Seven-headed Ser-

No. 328

pent, the Creator, gave seven great commands."

These two tablets tell us that these seven commands

were given to the Four Great Primary Forces. That these Forces were the executors of the Creator's commands throughout the Creation.

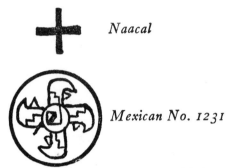

Naacal

Mexican No. 1231

"*The First Command:* 'Let the gases, which are scattered throughout space and without form and order, be brought together and out of them let worlds be formed.'

Mexican No. 339

Then the gases were brought together in the form of whirling masses."

"*The Second Command:* 'Let the gases solidify and let the earth be formed.' Then the gases solidified. Volumes were left on the outside of the crust, from which the waters and the atmosphere were to be formed; and volumes were left enveloped within the crust. Darkness prevailed, and there was no sound for as yet neither the atmosphere nor the waters were formed."

"The Third Command: 'Let the outside gases be separated and let them form the waters and the atmos-

Mexican No. 1267

phere.' And the gases were separated. One part went to form the waters, the remainder formed the atmosphere. The waters settled upon the face of the Earth so that no land appeared anywhere."

Naacal No. 10

"The gases which did not form the waters, went to form the atmosphere. And the shafts of the Sun met the shafts of the earth's light contained in the atmosphere, which gave birth to light. Then there was light upon the face of the Earth."

Naacal No. 11

"And the shafts of the Sun met the shafts of the Earth's heat which was contained in her atmosphere and gave it life. Then there was heat to warm the face of the earth."

Mexican No. 51

"*The Fourth Command:* 'Let the fires that are within the earth raise land above the face of the waters.' Then the fires of the underneath lifted the land on which the waters rested until the land appeared above the face of the waters—this was the dry land."

Naacal   *Naacal*   *Egyptian*   *Hindu*
No. 12   *No. 13*   *No. 1*   *No. 2*

Mexican No. 328

"*The Fifth Command:* 'Let life come forth in the waters.' And the shafts of the Sun met the shafts of the earth in the mud of the waters, and out of particles of mud formed cosmic eggs. From these eggs life came forth as commanded."

Naacal No. 13

"*The Sixth Command:* 'Let Life come forth on the land.' And the shafts of the Sun met the shafts of the earth in the dust of the land and out of particles of dust formed cosmic eggs. From these cosmic eggs life came forth as commanded." (What I have translated as arrows and shafts is the glyph $>$.)

"*The Seventh Command:* And when this was done, the Seventh Intellect said: 'Let us make man after our own *fashion* and let us endow him with powers to rule this earth.' Then the Seven-Headed Intellect, The Creator of All Things throughout the Universe, created man and placed within his body a *living, imperishable spirit,* and man became *like* the Creator in *intellectual* power."

What does the phrase "after our own fashion" mean? It certainly does not mean in the *image* of the Creator; for, a little farther on in the Sacred Writings, it says: "To man the Creator is incomprehensible. He can

Mexican Tablet No. 1584
Creation of the First Pair
Man and Woman

neither be *pictured* nor named, He is the Nameless."

If man were "in the image of God" he would be a picture of God; and, as God can neither be pictured nor named, being incomprehensible, the Bible has erred in translation by using the word "image."

"Like the Creator" unquestionably means, in intellect and mystic powers, for man possesses both.

Mexican Tablet No. 1584: This tablet reads:— "Man was created with the dual principle, male and female. The Creator caused this man to pass into a sleep (our death) and while he slept, the principles were severed by Cosmic Forces. When he awoke (born again) he was two—man and woman."

There are innumerable writings stating that man was created alone, and that woman was taken from a part of the original man. I shall quote a few prominent writings on the subject and also include some legends.

THE BIBLE.—*Genesis. 2. V. 21-22.*

"And the Lord God caused a deep *sleep* [Among the ancients death was called sleep: therefore, here sleep is equivalent to our death.] to fall upon Adam, and he slept: [that is he died] and He took one of his ribs, and closed up the flesh instead thereof. And the rib which the Lord God had taken from man, made he a woman, and brought her unto the man."

This is Ezra's translation of the writings of Moses 800 years after. Moses' writings were copies of the Naga in the language and writing of the Motherland and were only partially understood by Ezra who had not become a Master in the Chaldi in Babylonia before he was released from bondage and returned to his own land.

EGYPT.—Egypt obtained the Sacred Inspired Writings of Mu from two sources, in which the creation of woman appears. First, from India, brought by the Nagas when they made their first settlement at Maioo in Nubia, Upper Egypt. Second, from Atlantis, brought by the Mayas under the leadership of Thoth, who made his first settlement at Sais on the Nile Delta, Lower Egypt. This probably accounts for two versions of the Creation in the early chapters of the Bible. One was from the people who came from India—the other from the people who came from Atlantis, forming Upper and Lower Egypt.

HINDU.—The Sacred Inspired Writings of Mu were brought to India by the Naacals from the Motherland, and from India they were carried by the Naacals to the more recent colonies of Babylonia on the Euphrates and to Maioo in Upper Egypt.

CHALDEAN.—The Chaldean and Egyptian were therefore reflexes of the Hindu, and the Hindu a reflex of the Motherland: thus showing, definitely, that the legend of woman coming out of man originated in Mu, the Motherland.

HAWAII. PACIFIC ISLANDS.—The Hawaiians have a very ancient legend stating:—"*Taaroa* made man out of red earth *Araca,* and *breathed into his nostrils.* He made woman from man's bones and called her *Ivi.*"

THE CREATION

This part of the legend is identical with the Biblical and continues so throughout, except in unimportant details.

In the Polynesian language every letter in a word is pronounced: thus Ivi in Polynesian is pronounced *Eve-y*. Mu was destroyed about 12,000 years ago, so that this legend must have been orally handed down for at least 12,000 years.

THE GREEK LEGEND.—In all of their conceptions, the Greeks were always original. They gave a viewpoint on a subject different from all others, even to the creation of man and woman.

Plato says: "Human beings were originally created with the man and woman combined in one body. Each body had four arms and four legs. The bodies were round, and they rolled over and over, using the arms and legs to move them. By and by they began to treat the gods badly. They stopped their sacrifices and even threatened to roll up Mount Olympus to attack and overthrow the gods.

"One god said, 'Let us kill them all. They are dangerous.'

"Another said, 'No, I have a better idea. We will cut them in half. Then they will only have two arms and two legs; they won't be round. They won't be able to roll. Being multiplied by two, they will offer twice as many sacrifices, and what is the most important, each half will be so busy looking for the other half that they will not have time to bother us.' "

UIGHUR.—Plate I (between pages 160–1) coming from the ancient capital of the Uighurs, destroyed about 18,000 to 20,000 years ago—Chinese records say 19,000 years ago—is probably the oldest record of man being created with the dual principle.

There are in this world those, the spiritual part of whose brains are so finely keyed to each other, that words are unnecessary to express the feelings of one towards the other when they *first* meet. These possibly are the two halves of man and woman which in bygone times made one soul. All the past is bridged at a glance. The divine, pure love for one another leaps into life again on the instant. Many modern writers have vulgarly termed this "the man call." It is not the man call; it is the souls' call, mates. The "man call" is materialism. Materialism has nothing to do with it, because the call is spiritual.

Again, two persons, meeting for the first time, may or may not take a dislike to one another. One of them at least may take a dislike to the other and mistrust the other for no apparent reason. This is popularly termed "first impressions." Probably if their past incarnations could be recalled and they could see all that happened in them, the question would be answered.

A glyph, generally a circle but sometimes oblong with two parallel lines drawn through its center dividing it into three parts as shown Cut. 1 (Niven's Mexican Tablet No. 2379), is a common universal symbol.

It is found among the cliff writings of our western

states, in inscriptions on the Mexican Pyramid at Xochicalco, in the Maya writings of Yucatan. It appears in a writing on Inscription Rock, northeast Brazil

Cut 1. Mexican No. 2379

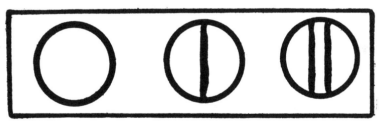

Cut 2. A paragraph in the Sacred Inspired Writings
(Naacal writing)

near the boundary of British Guiana, and in other various American carvings. It occurs in the ancient writings of the Uighurs, Hindus, Babylonians and Egyptians.

In the Oriental Naacal writings of the Sacred Inspired Writings, The Books of the Golden Age, it is one
of three glyphs forming a paragraph. (See Cut. 2.) The
paragraph reads: (◯ Hun)—The Creator is one.
(⬤ Lahun, two)—He is two in one. (⬤ Mehen,
man)—These two engendered the son, mehen—man.
It is thus shown that the glyph ⬤ refers to the Creation of man, and by the ordinary extensions given these
very ancient symbols, includes producing a continuance
of, et cetera.

Lao Tzu in *Tao te King,* a Chinese book written about
600 B. C. just before the time of Confucius, we read:
"Reason Tao *made* One. One *became* two. Two *produced* three. From these three, *all* mankind descended."

In deciphering and translating this glyph, collected
from many parts of the earth, I have invariably found
that, in the ancient explanation of it, three words persist
in every translation of it, viz: *made or created, became*
and *produced;* thus:

The Creator *created* man, man *became* two, these
two *produced* three, clearly in each case showing and
defining the form of the steps in progression, and the
difference between each step.

An ancient glyph which by the ancients was called
"The Mysterious Writing" is an esoteric temple writing, a numeral writing, conveying the same meaning
and conception as the Mexican Tablet No. 2379.

THE CREATION

THE MYSTERIOUS WRITING.—The Mysterious Writing consisted of either six small circles or six small disks, placed so as to form a triangle, pyramid or keystone. The rows are so placed that they count—one, two, three.

Cut 3.
The Mysterious Writing

The two figures forming Cut 3 are written with the Naga form of numerals. Sometimes the Nagas used circles, at other times disks; this appears to have been optional, dependent on the taste of the writer.

The Uighurs, generally, used a bar or line to express their numerals. I find their expression of the one, two and three most frequently written thus

or ❘ ❘❘ ❘❘❘ .

KARA INSCRIPTION IN BRAZIL.—On a large prairie-like plain in the northeastern part of Brazil near the boundary of British Guiana stands an immense rock with many smooth faces which are literally covered with very old inscriptions in the characters of the ancient Karas or Carians.

The following is one of the inscriptions with its deciphering and translation:

1. This is a universal symbol found in the writings of all ancient people.

2. The Northern or Uighur form of writing the numeral 1. (Cara or Karian pattern)

3. Numeral 2.

4. Numeral 3. This glyph is specialized by not having one end closed which gives it a special significance.

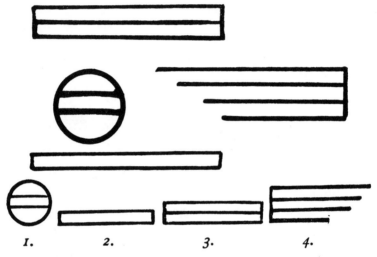

1.   *2.*   *3.*   *4.*

The Legend: One *became* two. Two *produced* three. From these three the life was *continued* on.

The continuation is shown in the glyph for numeral 3 where the ends of the bars are left open. The ancients designated by unattached ends that unfinished work was being carried on.

It may be well to note here that the Cara glyph for 1, an enclosed bar, was the Naga glyph for 5. All Naga counts were made up of 5's; thus ten would be two or twice five. Ten being the numeral symbol of the Infinite, was never used. As the symbol of the Infinite it was looked upon as being too sacred.

I have here shown a South American inscription composed of a symbol or vignette with its meaning given in script. This, to a great extent, follows the character of the Sacred Inspired Writings of Mu; further, it is unquestionable that this passage was taken from the Sacred Writings for on the other side of the world comes the Motherland. In China we find Lao Tzu in *Tao te King,* using virtually the same words about 600 B. C. which he took from the Sacred Writings of the Motherland.

XOCICALCO PYRAMID—MEXICO.—On this celebrated pyramid there are many inscriptions. I have selected one which appears to me to be relative to the creation of the first pair.

Uighur writing

1st Line. Numerals one, two and three with their hidden meaning as previously given.

2nd Line. Includes the Uighur glyph for man having the dual principle. Man before he became divided.

3rd Line. Includes man as the male principle only

Ʀ (When *mankind* was referred to, the Uighur plain letter M ⊓ was given.)

1.   2.   3.   4.

The evolution of the Uighur letter M
1. Naga Mu. 2. Uighur Mu. 3. Second changing the right leg to be the longer. 4. Third, the last pattern handed down to the Chinese.

THE WATERS—THE MOTHER OF LIFE.—Throughout all ancient writings the waters are referred to as "The Mother of Life." Thus it is shown that the ancients knew perfectly well what is confirmed by geology today: that is, the first life on earth was marine life, that is, it first appeared in the waters (see Plate III).

To think that life first appeared in the waters is not only reasonable, but it was imperative according to natural laws that it should do so; for, life can only commence at a temperature below 200° F. I have been unable to produce life at over 175° F.

During the earth's cooling, the waters were always a step in advance of the rocks in cooling; therefore the waters being in advance of the rocks in cooling were down to a temperature where life could make a start before life could start among the rocks, or at the best hot, rocky, gravelly sand with little or no actual soil.

The first life that appeared on this earth were tiny microscopical marine grasses and lichens. These were destined to become the foundation stones of *The House of Life—Nature's lives* and so the house was built upon them until *Man, the Special Creation,* came to form the Divine coping stone.

Fig. 1.

Fig. 2.

Various serpents are mentioned in the ancient writings, each one symbolizing something different from the others. These ancient Serpent Symbols are divided into two classes:

1. The adorned Serpent symbolizing the Creative Attribute of the Deity.

2. Plain unadorned Serpents were symbols of the waters. The symbolic water symbol was called *Khan.*

KH   A   N

Fig. 1. This serpent is one of the vignettes appearing in the Sacred Writings—Fifth Command. As this serpent has a nest of eggs within her coils, it is permissible to assume that this creation refers to various forms of marine life.

Mexican Tablet, No. 328. This serpent symbolizes

actual first life in the waters, therefore the first life on earth.

Fig. 2. Is the usual form of the water symbol, without any additions, such as eggs, et cetera.

Egyptian Vignette

HORUS IN COMBAT WITH APHOPHIS.—This vignette comes from an Egyptian papyrus dating about 3,000 B. C. It depicts Horus the symbol of the Sun in combat with Aphophis the waters.

This illustration plainly shows a great difference in the teachings from the original that are found in the Sacred Writings and which are repeated and confirmed in the Mexican Tablet No. 328. There the scientific account is given. In the Egyptian a symbol is given without the explanation. The Mexican Tablet is at least 7,000 years older than this Egyptian vignette.

But Egypt did not stand alone in this obtuse teaching:—the Greeks had their Apollo, the Sun, killing the Serpent Python, the waters. The Hindus had Krishma killing the Serpent Anatha, the waters, and the Chaldeans had Belmarduk, the Sun, overcoming Tiamat, the waters.

Chaldean tablet found in the library of the palace of King Assurbanipal: "At a time when neither the heavens above nor the earth below existed, there was the watery abyss: the first of seed, the mistress of the depths, the mother of the Universe.

"The waters covered everything; no product had ever been gathered nor was there any sprout seen, aye, the very gods had not yet come into being.

"The gods are preparing for a grand contest against the monster known as Tiamat, the waters; the god Belmarduk overthrows Tiamat."

Tiamat is a Naga word meaning water everywhere, nowhere land. Belmarduk was the Babylonian name for the Sun as the celestial orb and not as the symbol Ra.

From the foregoing it appears to be that the first two extracts correspond to the Mexican Tablet No. 339, and the last to the advent of life on earth. Some connecting tablets are evidently missing.

In the Sacred Writings of Mu it is plainly shown that

there was *no combat or fighting.* That it was the commingling of forces in connection with elementary matter
that produced the results and that the Natural Law regarding the creation of Life had only been followed.

The savages and semi-savages of the South Sea
Islands have legends among themselves showing that
they understand the workings of the Forces better than
the myths taught by the Egyptians, Greeks, Hindus and
Chaldeans, which go to prove that these myths were
bred after Mu went down and the South Sea Islands became isolated from the rest of the world.

The South Sea Islanders explain that all creations
are the result of marriages (commingling) between
gods (Forces), which is correct. Theirs is the original
explanation orally handed down for 12,000 years, and
wonderfully well they have kept it.

Of course there are divergences from the original,
but when one considers the time they have been orally
passed on from father to son, *it is a miracle* that the differences are so immaterial; but they have had no unscrupulous priesthoods to tamper with the great things
left behind.

THE BIBLE.—Referring to the Bible again, and to
show how extremely old some parts of it are, those
which came out of the Sacred Inspired Writings, I
will call attention to a few facts.

Moses without question bases his religious laws on
the Pure Osirian as taught by Thoth. Take for instance
the ten commandments. In the Great Hall of Truth of

Osiris there are placed forty-two gods in a row, to ask the soul when it enters this Judgment Hall forty-two *questions* regarding the life of the material body in which it had dwelt.

Moses took these forty-two questions and in a condensed form made forty-two *commands* out of them which he condensed to ten commands. This drastic change made by Moses was unquestionably necessary to meet the condition into which his people had fallen. Moses changed nothing in conception, he simply made more emphatic how they must live their lives here on earth. He applied these laws to the living directly instead of to the dead. The ten commandments, however, are found in the Sacred Inspired Writings of Mu more than 70,000 years ago, only in the form of questions instead of commands.

But the Jews were not the only people who had a conception that their religious laws came directly from the Supreme God through some agent, and this may be so for we have no record who wrote the writings of Mu and it is distinctly stated they are Sacred and Inspired. Who was the inspired one? What was his name?

Diodorus Siculus says:

"The Egyptians claim that their religious laws were given to Menevis by Hermes.

"The Cretans held that their religious laws were given by Minos who received them from Zeus.

"The Lycedaemonians claimed that theirs were the gift of Apollon to Lykurgus.

"The Aryans were given theirs by Zathraustes who received them from the Good Spirit.

"The Getae claim that Zamolxis obtained theirs from the goddess Hestia.

"The Jews claim that Moses received theirs from Iao."

The inscriptions on the old Akkadian ruins of Babylonia, clearly express the feelings and ideas of these people 10,000 to 15,000 years ago about man and the creation. They believed man was a special creation and showed how he came into being. They clearly indicate that God was the Creator and that His Forces control the Universe and all therein. This is corroborated by the Sacred Inspired Writings, the writings on the Mexican Tablets, and the cliff writings of North America. All support the fact that the first religion was pure Monotheism, that the Creator created all things and today is controlling the Universe with all the life throughout it.

Writings from western Thebes by one Amenemopet (Priest) are word for word the same as the Proverbs written by Solomon. These writings are dated several hundreds of years before Solomon was born.

Solomon was a scholar and reproduced these wonderful epics. Further, it is clearly shown that besides being a Jew he was an Osirian—the building of his temple showed it. Wherever possible in its construction, Solomon carried out the most minute details, shown in the symbolical Hall of Truth, Osiris presiding.

The Porch especially is noteworthy, for it has the two

pillars with identically the same names and the same decorative ornamentations.

Without question Solomon knew and appreciated that his religion was nothing more or less than the Pure Osirian religion, arranged and modified to suit the people of his times.

CHAPTER V

SYMBOLS USED IN RELIGIOUS
TEACHINGS

THE symbols which were used in the religious teachings of early man are popularly known as the Sacred Symbols.

When symbols were first used it was to concentrate man's mind on the Infinite One, so that by keeping his eyes on the symbol no outside sights or sounds might call off his attention from the object of worship. Man was most carefully taught that the symbol itself was not to be worshipped; the symbol was only a picture to keep his mind from wandering. He was carefully taught that there was only *One* Deity, but that One Deity had many attributes which looked after health and strength, rain and sunshine, crops; in fact, after the whole welfare of mankind.

In the beginning three symbols only were used. When these were understood, they were compounded and others added, and as time grew so did the number of symbols, also their complexity, until we come down to Egypt about 3,000 or 4,000 years ago, when there was such a riot of symbols scarcely one temple understood the meaning of half the symbols used in another.

The three original symbols which I have referred to are: *The Circle, The Equilateral Triangle* and *The Square.*

THE CIRCLE.—The Circle is a picture of the Sun and was the symbol of the Infinite One. As it embraced all of His attributes it was the Monotheistic Symbol. Being the Monotheistic Symbol it was considered the Most Sacred Symbol of all. According to legend, the Sun was selected for this symbol because it was the most powerful object that came within the sight and understanding of man at that time.

The circle having no beginning and no ending also symbolized:—everlasting, without end and infinity.

Before very long it is shown that the circle was being used to symbolize so many things that it became necessary to specialize the circle when using it as the Monotheistic Symbol of the Deity. The Nagas made an addition by placing a dot in the center of the circle. The Uighurs added a smaller circle within, making it a double circle.

Papyrus Anana: This is one of the most beautiful Egyptian writings that I have come across. Anana was chief scribe and king's companion to the gentle Seti II about 1320 B. C.

"Behold! is it not written in this roll? Read, ye who

shall find in the days unborn, if your gods have given you the skill. Read, O children of the future, and learn the secrets of the past, which to you is so far away, and yet in truth so near.

"Men do not live once only and then depart hence forever; they live many times in many places, though not always in this world. That between each life there is a veil of darkness.

"The doors will open at last, and show us all the chambers through which our feet wandered from the beginning.

"Our religion teaches us that we live on eternally. Now eternity having no end, can have had no beginning —*it is a circle;* therefore, if one be true, namely that we live on forever, it would seem that the other must be true also: namely, that we *have always lived.*

"To men's eyes God has many faces, and each one swears that the one he sees is the only true God. Yet they are all wrong, for all are true.

"Our Kas, which are our spiritual selves, show them to us in various ways. Drawing from the infinite well of wisdom that is hidden in the being of every man, gives us glimpses of the truth, as they give us, who are instructed, *power to work marvels.*

"The Spirit should not be judged by the body or the god by his house.

"Among the Egyptians the Scarabaeus Beetle is no god, but a symbol of the Creator, because it rolls a ball of mud between its feet and sets therein its eggs to hatch as the Creator rolls the world around which seems to be round causing it to produce life.

"All gods send their gift of love upon this earth, without which it would cease to be. My faith teaches me more clearly perhaps than yours, that life does not end with death, and therefore that love, being life's soul, must endure while it endures.

"The strength of the invisible tie will bind two souls together long after the world is dead.

"The spirits or souls of one incarnation possibly may meet again in another incarnation, and may be drawn together as if by a magnet but for what cause neither knows.

"Man comes into being many times, yet knows nothing of his past lives; except occasionally some daydream or a thought carries him back to some circumstance of a previous incarnation. He cannot, however, determine in his mind when or where the circumstance occurred only that it is something familiar. In the end, however, all of his various pasts will reveal themselves."

Various forms and modifications of the Sun as Ra are to be found in the ancient writings.

Fig. 1. The Original Monotheistic Symbol of The Deity.

Fig. 2. A subsequent change made by the Nagas.

Fig. 3. A subsequent change made by the Uighurs.

Fig. 4. Part of the headdress of some of the Egyptian gods.

Fig. 5. This generally appears as a red sphere on tops of pillars and monuments to the dead.

The foregoing Suns are all the Monotheistic Symbol of the Deity and among the ancients was called Ra.

I will now take some pictures of the Sun appearing in ancient writings as the celestial orb and *not* as Ra the Monotheistic symbol.

Fig. A. Is an eight-ray'd Sun. This was Mu's symbol on her Royal Escutcheon. The name in the Motherland of the Sun as the celestial orb was—Kin. In Egypt the name was—Horus. In Greece—Apollo and in Babylonia—Belmarduk, et cetera.

Fig. B. A Sun with rays all around it represented the Sun at his meridian in mid-heavens.

Fig. C. A rising Sun with rays, half the orb above the horizon, was the symbol on the escutcheon of a colonial empire of Mu.

Fig. D. A Sun with half the orb above the horizon without rays had a dual symbolization. It was the symbol of the setting Sun. It was also the symbol of a colony of Mu, before it became a colonial empire.

Fig. E. The Lands of the West in darkness. The three-pointed figure is Mu's numeral symbol as the Lands of the West. The Sun above without rays says that no light reaches Mu—she is in darkness. A vignette from the "Book of the Dead."

Fig. F. The Sacrifice of Mu. The Lotus above is Mu's floral symbol; being shown withered and dying it symbolizes Mu as being dead. A rayless Sun stands between Mu and the altar; therefore Mu is dead in the region of darkness—on the altar as a sacrifice.

Fig. G. "Peaks only remain above the water." Mu is here depicted as being dead and in darkness with only points or peaks remaining above the water. Kin no longer shines upon her. Vignette from the Egyptian "Book of the Dead."

THE EQUILATERAL TRIANGLE.—The equilateral triangle has a dual significance, dependent upon where and how it is used. Its origin dates back as solving to primitive man the emersion of the three lands which formed the Land of Mu—the Lands of the West.

The Lands of the West consisted of a huge continental island and two small ones, separated from the big one by narrow seas, called in the Egyptian "canals." Tradition says that the big continental island was first emerged and that the two small islands were subsequently emerged at different periods. It was to explain this phenomenon, of the three lands coming up at different periods, that the triangle was selected.

The equilateral triangle has three equal sides joined to one another and forming a single unbroken line without ends.

It was pointed out to primitive man that it was the same Creator that raised all three lands, each land being raised by separate commands: Thus there were not three Creators but only one. Apparently, to make it more understandable, each was raised by a separate attribute.

This formed the first Triune Godhead whereon have been built the enormous number of Pantheons that have permeated all ages. The conception of a Triune Godhead has been handed down from the beginning of religious teachings and still remains with us.

An equilateral triangle symbolized the Creator, and, as the Creator dwells in Heaven, the triangle must necessarily symbolize heaven also; for, where the Lord is, there is Heaven.

I find this verified among the Egyptian symbols, as the glyph shows. Here we find the Monotheistic Symbol of the Deity within the triangle—within Heaven. Wherever or whenever the equilateral triangle is met with in *ancient* writings or inscriptions, it is either in reference to the Triune Godhead, or Heaven, or both.

At the time of Confucius, the Chinese Sage, about 500 B. C., in place of the triangle the Chinese used a glyph in the form of the present-day capital Y. This they called: "the Great Term," "the Great Unite," "the Great Y." "The Y has neither body nor shape, all that has body and shape was made by that which has no shape. The Great Term or the Great Unite comprehends three—One in three—and three in One."

THE FOUR-SIDED SQUARE.—The Four-sided Square completes the trilogy of the first and original Sacred Symbols.

The square was selected as a conventional symbol of the earth for apparently two reasons:—To prevent it from being confounded with the Sun whose picture was a circle; and for the purpose of teaching to primitive man the cardinal points North, South, East and West. Being drawn as a square gave the earth "four corners" which were to be explained as teaching developed. Later the four corners became the positions of the "Four Great Pillars," one of the many names given to the Four Great Primary Forces which emanate from the Creator. These Forces first evolved law and order out of chaos and darkness; then created the bodies of the Universe and all therein. They now continue and uphold the work that they have accomplished, hence the name of "Pillars" having been given to them. The next step was to appoint keepers for the Pillars. These were known as the Genii.

Apparently, when the meanings of the foregoing three symbols were learnt by primitive man, his next lesson was the compounding of these three symbols.

TRIANGLE WITH THREE STARS.— Fig 1. The triangle here symbolizes Heaven. The three stars within symbolize the three members of the Triune Godhead. The Triune Godhead dwells in Heaven.

TRIANGLE WITH FIVE STARS.— Fig 2. The triangle

symbolizes Heaven. The five stars within symbolize the full Godhead of Five, namely, the Deity and his Four Great Primary or Creative Forces. The Deity with His Great Forces dwells in Heaven.

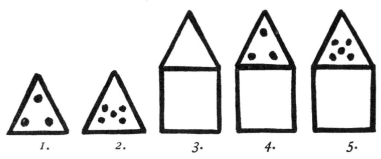

1.   2.   3.   4.   5.

A TRIANGLE SURMOUNTING A SQUARE. Fig. 3. This glyph is composed of the four-sided square the symbol of the earth, with the triangle symbol of Heaven surmounting it; thus showing Heaven above Earth. Above, in this case, does not refer to altitude in any way. It means: that Heaven is on a higher plane, where life is more perfect than here on earth. Thus this symbol depicts Heaven as being more perfect than earth, more blissful and happy.

A TRIANGLE SURMOUNTING A SQUARE AND THE TRIANGLE HAVING THREE STARS WITHIN.—Fig. 4. In this symbol there is an addition of three stars placed within the triangle, symbolizing that the Triune Godhead is in Heaven, above the Earth. This symbol is to be seen on the end wall of an end room of an ancient temple in Uxmal, Yucatan. This temple has been called "The Temple of Sacred Mysteries" because there is an inscription on a wall stating that the people came from

Mu and brought the Sacred Mysteries with them. In the room where this symbol appears, the postulant received his second degree.

The temple was built about 11,500 to 12,000 years ago as shown by an inscription on its walls which states, "that this temple was erected as a monument to Mu."

A TRIANGLE SURMOUNTING A SQUARE AND THE TRIANGLE HAVING FIVE STARS WITHIN.—Fig. 5. As previously stated five stars symbolize the full Godhead of Five—The Deity and His Four Great Primary Forces. This symbol is to be seen on the end of the wall of the opposite room to the one previously mentioned in the Temple of Sacred Mysteries at Uxmal. Here the postulant received his third degree, and was then prepared to enter the Holy of Holies.

This ends the compounding of the three original symbols.

The Sacred Symbols:—The circle, triangle, square and pentagon became the foundation of the wonderful geometrical knowledge attained in Mu and thoroughly entwined religion with science.

SYMBOLS OF MORTALITY.—A short space above the lintel of the entrance to the sanctuary of the Temple of Sacred Mysteries at Uxmal, Yucatan, is a cornice that surrounds the whole edifice. On it are sculptured the symbols of mortality which are many times repeated. The emblems of mortality occupied a very prominent place in ancient religion. It was extensively used by the Mayas, Quiches, Egyptians, Hindus and Babylonians and was found in the writings and inscriptions of all ancient lands.

The emblems of mortality were used in the ancient religious ceremonies to impress upon the postulant what his end would be and the end of all mortality, and with this end in view impress upon him constantly the necessity of living a life that would bring no terrors when the soul releases itself from the body to pass into the world beyond.

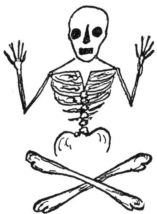

The Egyptian was a reflex of the Maya, and the Maya the teachings direct from the Motherland so that, from Egypt, we can get the original ceremonies with but immaterial changes. In the temple within the Great Pyramid was found in one of the chambers a sarcophagus with the emblems of mortality arranged alongside of it. The postulant was placed in the sarcophagus; here he was reminded that after his soul leaves his mortal body another life awaits him. This ceremony persists with the Freemasons today.

The TAU (*Ta-oo*).—The Tau is not only one of the most interesting, but it is one of the most ancient symbols, as it is found repeatedly in the oldest writings of the Motherland.

It is the symbol of both resurrection and emersion. Emersion is really only a resurrection of land. I know of no country on the face of the earth today that has not been under water several times—thus each time it was emersed it was resurrected.

The Tau

The name today is as it was in the Motherland—Tau; it was Tau then and it is Tau today. It is one of the very few words that has persisted through all time without a change in any way. The name means "the stars which bring the water." Ta—stars, and ha—water. The Marquesans today pronounce it "Ta-ha" (the pure Motherland pronunciation).

The Tau is the picture of the constellation, the Southern Cross, the most gorgeous group of stars appearing south of the equator. When the Southern Cross appeared at a certain angle over Mu, the rainy season commenced. The parched, dry land responded to the moisture from above. Leaves, flowers and fruit sprang forth upon tree and shrub. Seeds in the ground, that had been lying dead, germinated and sprang forth into life, en-

riching the land with golden grain. Mu became the land
of plenty. Life had been resurrected.

Fig. A.

Fig. A: This is an example, showing how the Mayas
often depicted the Tau as a tree, with two branches bearing flowers and fruit.

Fig. B.

Fig. B: This vignette comes from the Troano MS. It
describes the arrival of the rainy season in Mayax. The
figures are symbolical.

I give now three cuts that show the Tau symbolizing emersion.

The Emersion of Mu and the Advent of Man on Earth

Sacred Writings: This is a vignette from the Sacred Inspired Writings symbolizing Mu as the land emerged.

Naga Vignette: Children of Mu leaving the Motherland by water, the Tau is Mu emerged. This is from a Hindu carving 25,000 years old.

Naga Vignette: Children of Mu leaving the Mother-

Children of Mu leaving the Motherland by water

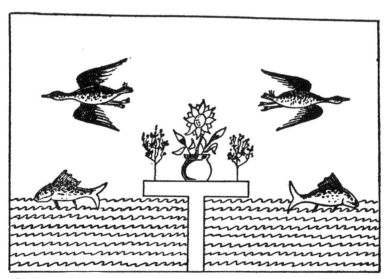

Children of Mu leaving the Motherland by air and by water

land by air and water. The Tau is Mu emerged. This is from a Hindu carving 25,000 years old.

THE DOUBLE TRIANGLE.—A pair of triangles bound together at their base, thus forming a double triangle, was the ancient symbol for an offering, and often appeared on the altar where offerings were made. These altars were generally in the form of the Tau, or had a Tau carved on the face of the altar. The rain brought by the Tau made offerings possible. These offerings, generally, were in the form of flowers or fruit, or products from the fields.

Before the destruction of Mu, sacrifices were unknown. Sacrifice was a word coined to describe the awful destruction of the beloved Motherland.

The general position in which the double triangle was placed was directly under the arms of the Tau, and in the ancient ritual these are supposed to say or read, "Place thine offering upon this altar."

THE TWO-SIDED SQUARE.—The two-sided square is known among the Masonic brotherhood as the two-sided or Mason's square. It is a very ancient glyph,

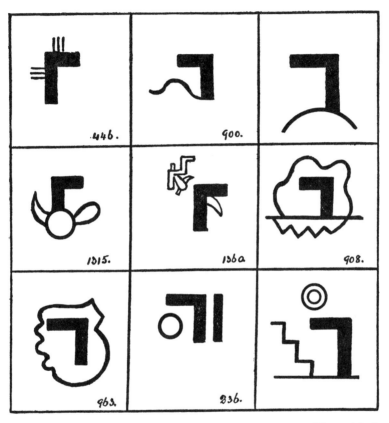

Group of Niven's Mexican Tablets showing the Two-sided Square

reading "Builder," and apparently was first used in the crosses symbolizing The Sacred Four when the name of the Great Builders of the Universe was given to them. This glyph was placed within the arm or loop of the cross which symbolized The Four Primary Forces, thus naming them "Builders."

The two-sided square is on many of Niven's Mexican tablets. I am giving a page of examples. In all of these tablets they are referring to the Sacred Four as "The Great Builders of the Universe." Down to the time of Mu's destruction, this symbol was used only to express builders as the name of the Creative Forces.

When, however, thousands of years afterwards, we enter Egypt, we find this symbol with a new vestment and a new name. Here it became the symbol of justice and uprightness.

It has always been thought that this symbol originated in Egypt but it goes back thousands of years beyond the commencement of Egyptian history. The two-sided square is a symbol which is constantly found in the Book of the Dead, also in various Egyptian papyrii. All seats where either gods or goddesses are shown sitting are composed of the two-sided square. In the Great Hall of Truth where Osiris is shown sitting in judgment his seat is composed of the two-sided square.

The people of Egypt were taught that this symbol of the two-sided square represented: "Right from wrong, to act on the square, to act rightly, to act justly, to act truthfully according to Maat." To only the initiated and

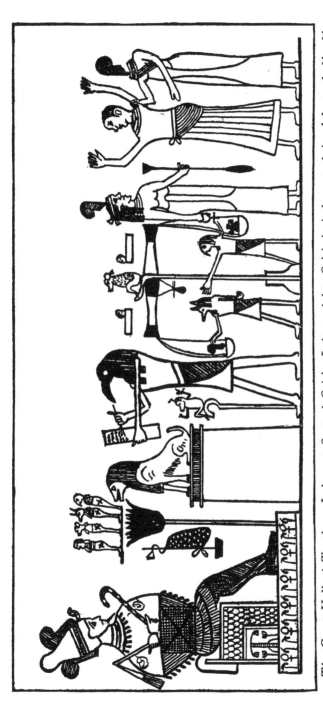

The Great Hall of Truth or Judgment Seat of Osiris. Left to right: Osiris in judgment chair. A leopard skin, his banner. Four genii over closed lotus flower, symbol of Mu. Great beast of Amenti. Thoth with Ibis head recording history of the deceased. Anubis with jackal's head and Horus with hawk's head weighing the heart in pair of scales against a feather. The deceased, hands aloft exposing his heart, being led into the Hall of Truth by a feather and being received by Maat, goddess of Truth. From the Egyptian "Book of the Dead," chapter 125.

the priesthood of Egypt was the actual meaning of this symbol known. This is shown by the title and symbol of the god Ptah. Two of his titles were "The Divine Artificer" and "The Divine Builder"; accompanying these titles was the two-sided square. In all of the designs of Egyptian Pillars, they symbolize the ancient and true meaning.

THE CUBE.—This symbol is especially interesting to Arch Masons. It is found in the 64th Chapter of the Book of the Dead which is the oldest and one of the most important chapters in this sacred volume, having been written by Thoth at Sais at the commencement of Egyptian history about 14,000 B. C. Translations of it vary somewhat but not materially. The following are some of the translations.

M. Paul Pierret translated one of the sentences from the Turin Copy as: "I am yesterday, and I know tomorrow, I am able to be born again."

London Papyrus reads: "I am yesterday, today and tomorrow."

The Ruberic says: "This chapter was found in the city of Khemennu upon a block of iron from the South which had been inlaid with letters of real Lapis Lazuli, under the foot of God during the reign of his majesty the King of the North and the South Men-Kan-Ra triumphant by the royal son Heru-Ta-Ta-f triumphant. He found it when he was journeying about to make an investigation of the temples. One Neskit was with him who was diligent in making him understand it, and he brought it to the King as a wonderful object. When he saw that thing of mystery which had never been seen or looked upon." London Papyrus dating 3733 B. C. *The cube* is what was found.

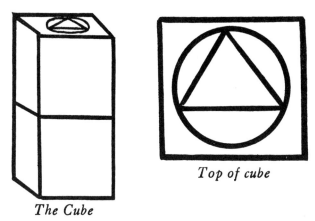

The Cube

Top of cube

M. *Paul Pierret's* translation from the Turin Papyrus: "This chapter was found out in Hermopolis on a brick of burnt clay, written in blue, under the feet of the god *Thoth*. The finding out at the time of King Menekara was made by Prince Har-titi-f in this place when he was travelling to inspect the temples. It related in itself a hymn which transported him into ecstasy. He brought it to the King's chariot as soon as he saw *what was drawn on the cube*—a great mystery."

Papyrus Mes-em-neter dated 4266 B. C.: "This chapter was found in the foundation of a plinth of the shrine of the Divine Hennu Boat by the chief mason in the time of the King of the North and the South Hesepti triumphant, and it is there directed that it shall be recited only by one who is ceremoniously clean and pure."

THE SACRED SYMBOLS OF MU

THE INTERLACED TRIANGLES.—The crossed triangle is an exceedingly old symbol. The oldest record of it that I have is in the Cosmogonic Diagram of the Motherland which is the mother of all cosmogonic

The Divine Hennu Boat

The flight of the soul to the region of incarnation. The deceased sailing his bark through the field of stars to Amenti, the domain of Osiris, for judgment and reincarnation.

diagrams. I did not find it in any of the Sacred Writings which I read, but that is no criterion, nor does it say that it does not appear in the Sacred Writings. There are over ten thousand tablets covering these writings. I have only seen about three thousand out of the ten.

The figure shows a central circle enclosed within a pair of triangles crossed and interwoven. Again the two triangles are enclosed within an outer circle which leaves twelve divisions between the two circles. The central symbol, the circle, is the monotheistic symbol of the Deity; the triangle of heaven, and the outer circle the Universe. The twelve divisions between the two

140

circles are gates, "The twelve gates to heaven." Each gate was a virtue, and these twelve gates must be opened by the twelve virtues before heaven could be entered. Among the twelve virtues were first of all Love; then followed Faith, Hope, Charity, et cetera.

THE FEATHER.—The feather is another of the very prominent Ancient Sacred Symbols; it symbolized Truth.

Three feathers adorned the Crown of Mu. Three feathers were the ornament on the head piece of Ra Mu, the King High Priest of Mu—Niven's Mexican Stone Tablet No. 1780.

We find feathers as symbols among the Mayas, the difference in color denoting the rank of the wearer. In Mu yellow was the color for royalty, blue for the priesthood and red for soldiers and nobility. In these ancient times yellow appears to have been the royal color throughout the world. A dark blue is the mourning color in the Orient today. Research shows that this color was adopted when Mu was sacrificed, and corresponds with the color of her burial shroud—the blue waters of the Pacific Ocean.

The feathers worn by the North American Indian today is a relic which he has inherited from his forefathers. Whether they know the original meaning of the feather, I cannot say. When on the warpath, however, they color the ends of their feathers red, corresponding with the red feathers of the soldiers and nobility of Mu.

In Egypt, however, we find more extensive informa-

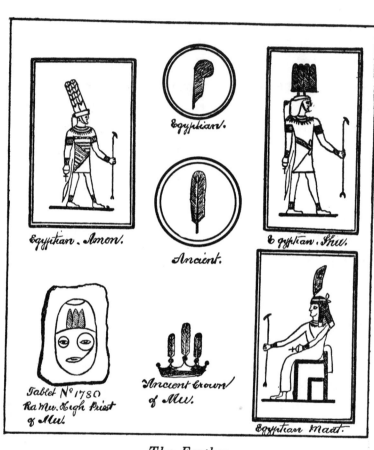

Egyptian.

Ancient.

Egyptian. Amon.

Egyptian. Shu.

Tablet Nº 1780
Ra Mu. High Priest
of Mu.

Ancient Crown
of Mu.

Egyptian Maat.

The Feather
Symbol of Truth

tion about the feather. In the early Egyptian times, as in Mu, a straight feather was used. About the time of Menes a curled ostrich feather was used on all new symbolizations. The curled feather is in the headdress of Osiris and Maat, and in the Great Hall of Truth an ostrich feather is shown as being weighed against the heart of the deceased, the feather symbolizing Truth.

Legend says that the feather was selected to symbolize Truth because a puff of wind blows it away. Truth is just as liable and easy to be frightened away as the feather is to be blown away.

The ancient name for the feather was Kukum, Ku or Kuk. Among the Mayas of North America we find a serpent called Kukul Khan which translated would be Khan—king, Kuk—feather, and ul—covered; so that a free translation would be: The King of Serpents which is covered with feathers. This corresponds with the Quiche Maya as recorded in their Sacred Book the Popol Vuh.

Pillars as sacred symbols are of an extremely ancient origin. My personal opinion is they date back to the *first* temple ever erected for the worship of the Infinite One and that was more than 70,000 years ago. The Pillar is one of the multitude of symbols which symbolize the Four Great Creative Forces. They were first used at the doorway or entrance to the temple. They were specialized in their construction and shapes. From various old tablets and fallen ruins I have reconstructed a pair as they were erected 20,000 years ago.

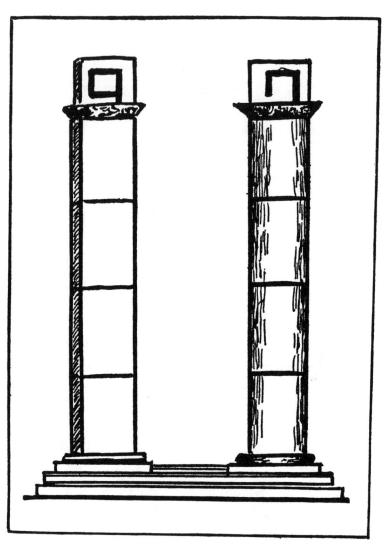

A Pair of Ancient Pillars

A Pair of Ancient Pillars: The pillar on the left was square and capped with the glyph ▢ strength. The right hand pillar was round and capped with the glyph ⌐ which in a general way means established, built up, and by extension, finished, accomplished, dependent on how and where used. Both pillars were in

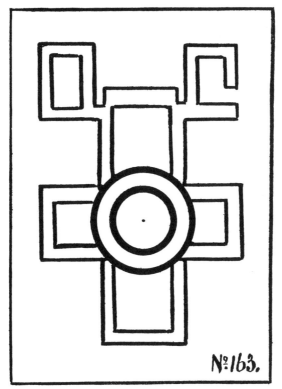

Pillar Cross

four sections, to correspond with the Four Great Primary Forces, the Four Great Gods, et cetera.

A Pillar Cross: The four arms of this cross are in

shape like the ancient glyph for Pillar. Connecting them all is shown their source, the great Creator. ◉

The upper pillar, or arm of the cross, is capped with two glyphs ☐ strength. ⊓ establish. Thus, this cross reads "The Pillars have been established in strength."

N⁰ 50.

Temple Porch with Two Pillars

Temple Porch with two Pillars: Niven's Mexican Stone Tablet No. 50, over 12,000 years old.

This temple has a dedication over the center of the

146

arch, the hieratic letter H ▯ in the alphabet of Mu. This was the alphabetical symbol of the Four Creative Forces. So this temple was dedicated to the Four Great Primary Forces. Below are shown two pillars, each one has four sections ☰ the numeral four (Uighur form) corresponding to the four Primary Forces. The left hand pillar is capped with the glyph ☐ strength, and the right hand one with the glyph ⊓ establish.

The ground plan of this temple which is on another tablet shows the left hand pillar to be square and the right hand one round.

A very old written record, dating back to about 11,000 years, comes from the Greek, and refers to the pillars of the temple dedicated to Poseidon of Atlantis.

The foregoing I think clearly establishes the antiquity of pillars as sacred symbols, with their shapes and meanings.

I shall now pass on to the Egyptians of much more recent time, taking the period of about 1,000 to 4,500 B. C.

Egyptian Pillars: This is a group of pillars taken from the Book of the Dead and various Egyptian Papyrii. By these it will be seen that the Egyptians did not adhere to the patterns and details of the ancients, but rather made a display of their imagination and artistry. Pillars came to Egypt with both tides of colonists, the Eastern Line brought them and the Western Line

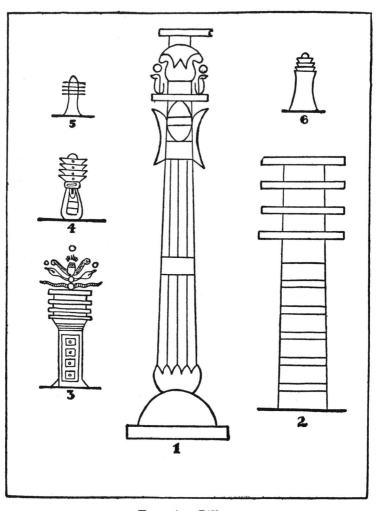

Egyptian Pillars

brought them and between the two, new conceptions of what pillars ought to be developed.

The Egyptians called them Tat Pillars. They are, however, better known throughout the world as Totem Pillars.

The Egyptians called one pillar "Tat" which in their language means "in strength." The other pillar they called "Tattu" which means "to establish," and when conjoined, "In strength this place is established for ever." The Egyptians considered the figure of a Tat an emblem of strength and stability.

It will be noticed that all of the pillars in this group carry four horizontal bars, in this way symbolizing the Four Great Primary Forces, or, as they were more wont to call them:—"The Four Great Gods."

The entrance to Amenti taken from the papyrus Anana, one of the most beautiful papyri I have ever seen. In Egyptian mythology, two Tats form the entrance to Tattu. Tattu is the gateway to the region where the mortal soul is blended with an immortal spirit and "established in the mysteries of Amenti for ever."

In the porch or entrance to King Solomon's Temple two special pillars were erected.

I Kings. Chap. 7, Verses 21–22. "And he set up the pillars in the porch of the temple, and he set up the right pillar, and called the name thereof Jachin, and he set up the left pillar, and called the name thereof Boaz."

At the entrance of King Solomon's Temple, and at the Osirian Great Hall of Truth, two pillars were

*Entrance to Tattu in Amenti (Egyptian) Showing the Two
Symbolic Pillars*

erected standing perpendicularly. In each case they have identically the same meanings, language considered, with identically the same names. Beyond this the ornamentation on the pillars—lily work—are also the same: showing that King Solomon's pillars were a complete copy of the pillars at the Great Hall of Truth; and while both change the pattern of the pillars that they both retained their original meaning: that is, they symbolized the work of the Four Great Primary Forces.

North American Indian: The Indians of our Northwestern states and of western Canada erect Totem Poles and hold ceremonies at their base. I have been unable to get anything about them except legend: but these legends and carvings on the Totem Poles strongly confirm the fact that the forefathers of those Indians came from Mu, and from that part of the Motherland where the bird was their symbol of the Creator.

The Maoris of New Zealand: A common practice of the Maoris of New Zealand is to erect Totem Poles or Pillars at the main entrance to their villages.

The Karangs of Java: Forbes in writing says:—"In Java is a tribe called Karangs, supposed to be the descendants of the aborigines of the island, whose old men and youths, four times a year repair secretly, in procession, to a sacred grove in a dense forest, the old men to worship, the youths to see and learn the mysteries of their forefathers.

"In this grove are the ruins of terraces laid out in

quadrilateral enclosures, the boundaries of which are marked by blocks of stone, or fixed in the ground. Here and there on the terraces are prominent monuments, *erect pillars,* and especially noteworthy, *a pillar erect within a square.*

"Here these despised and secluded people follow the rites and customs that have been handed down to them from their forefathers through vastly remote ages (about 12,000 years) repeating with superstitious awe a litany which they do not understand or comprehend. This very litany is found in the Egyptian Book of the Dead."

The Israelites in Egypt: While in Egypt the Israelites had two pillars of red brick at the entrance of their poor little temples. In many of their synagogues today, they erect two pillars at the entrance and say they symbolize the legendary pillars of fire and smoke that accompanied them during their exodus. What did their Egyptian Pillars symbolize?

Atlantis: Plato the Greek philosopher informs us that:—"The people of Atlantis gathered every fifth and sixth year alternately and with sacrifices of bulls swore to observe the sacred inscriptions carved on the *pillars of the temple."*

Troano MS: I have found the following mistranslations in the Troano MS Plate. ▭. This has been translated "Can the King." The correct translation is "The Four Pillars of the Earth." ▭ is the hieratic

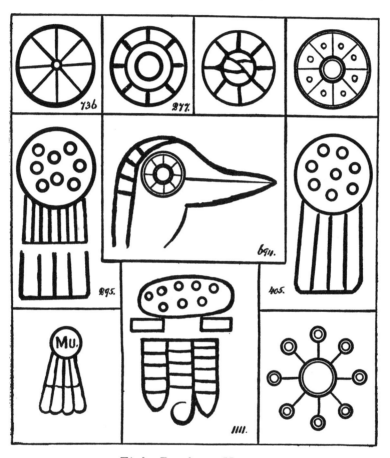

Eight Roads to Heaven

letter M in the Motherland's alphabet. The alphabetical symbol for mother, earth, land, et cetera, ● or ○ is the symbol for a pillar when the actual pillar is not shown; therefore, this glyph reads:—"The four pillars at the four corners of the earth." The whole of this plate is a mistranslation.

THE EIGHT ROADS TO HEAVEN.—The eight Roads to Heaven was a religious symbolic teaching which I first found in the Cosmogonic Diagram of Mu which attests its great antiquity. In this Cosmogonic Diagram it was used to show man how he must live on this earth to be prepared to pass into the world beyond when his call came. The eight Roads to Heaven was not an actual conception; it was a symbolic teaching, religious in character. These special teachings were unquestionably universal, as they are found among ancient people throughout the world. Such form of teaching must have been very popular since there were so many designs of symbols for it. Every ancient people appear to have had their own idea as to what design and figure best symbolized the eight Roads to Heaven.

THE LIFE SYMBOL—CRUX ANSATA OR ANKH.—Although known now as an Egyptian symbol only, like the Scarab it is very old. It is found in the writings of the

First Civilization, also carved on the stones of the North American cliff dwellers or their predecessors. The Life Symbol is a compound of two symbols. The O loop at the top symbolizes a mouth or gateway. It was from the Egyptian that the symbol of Venus, the looped cross, originated, and with its adoption a new vestment was given to it. With Venus it symbolized the triumph of the spirit over bodily matter, the soul over materialism. Venus was the Roman and Aphrodite the Greek. We find, among the Egyptian relics, that many of the symbols were very much ornamented. In the ancient writings I have only come upon plain, unornamented ones: all of the Egyptian were, however, not ornamented. As an example is the base on which the seat of Osiris rests in the Great Hall of Truth. Here it is many times repeated. Among the cliff dwellers or their predecessors, there is a tendency to curve the perpendicular member of the cross, thus ♀, which has led many archaeologists astray, inducing them to give the glyph an erroneous meaning.

THE ROADWAY OF THE SOUL.—I have found in my wanderings two figures prominently placed, but never came across the name by which they are called. As they are generally found on the outside of, and on the walls and ceilings of, burial chambers, I have given them the name as shown in the above caption. Some day perhaps their correct name may be known, then this temporary name can be abandoned.

For many years the spiral figure, Plate IV, has

been a puzzle to me, as it has been found all along the line of the great Uighur migration. The picture I am showing comes from New Grange, County Meath, Ireland.

The figure is either an explanation of the esoteric or hidden meaning of the hieratic letter N in Mu's alphabet, or the letter itself, highly embellished, I cannot say which. After a careful study of many of the writings of Mu in which the letter N appears, I find a slight variation in them. Sometimes they are formed thus ⌇, sometimes thus ⌇ . The difference is that in one the ends are left open—in the other they are closed—there are no ends. As there are no ends, the figure becomes a continuous line, returning to the starting point, and proceeding on as it can find no place to stop. It is therefore equivalent to a circle, which has no beginning or end.

In the picture shown from New Grange it will be seen the spirals have no ends, but when the center is reached the line returns on itself. There is no starting point in either of the spirals and no end given, consequently, these spirals are also the equivalent of a circle.

In the Sacred Writings of Mu we are told man's soul lives on until finally it reaches the source of its origin. *Ana.*, 1320 B. C., Egyptian Papyrus: "If we live on we must continue for ever, and if we continue for ever, like the circle and eternity, man had no beginning."

Here we find two ancient references to man's soul

having no end nor beginning. These spirals have no end or beginning and are generally found, associated with the passing on of the soul, in burial chambers of the material body. A careful study of the symbol and where and under what circumstances it is found leads me to the belief that:—These hitherto unreadable spiral symbols give the hidden meaning of the hieratic letter N—Mu's alphabet; that they are intended to depict the continuance of the soul from one cycle to another, from one incarnation to another, eventually ending whence it came. In the New Grange picture which I have shown there are three spirals all running into each other without an end. I take it that the third spiral is meant to indicate the passing of the soul into the world beyond or maybe to some other body in the Universe specially prepared to receive it.

On the walls of New Grange there are carved other symbols, spirals, squares, zig-zags, et cetera.

@ A spiral with an end pointing to the right is an ancient Uighur symbol meaning, "going to somewhere." It is also found in Mexico and among the North American Indians.

@ A spiral with an end pointing left is the corresponding symbol, saying, "coming from."

□ ◇ The original cosmogonic form or picture of the earth was a square. When placed flat it symbolized the earth. When placed on end it was to show the four cardinal points and in reference to the Four Pillars.

A square within a square placed on end symbolizes that something has gone from it.

Is the Uighur mountain and Chinese Yo; it is equivalent to the triangle. Freely read, "ascended."

A zig-zag or herring-bone with the points defined is the universal ancient symbol for a tank fire, an abyss of molten fire without flames, prominent in Egyptian symbology.

All these glyphs are on the stones of New Grange. I would not attempt to write a legend without seeing the stones personally. No draughtsman ever draws these ancient figures *as they are identically shown* on the stones. This has been my experience. Consequently no reading, or possibly an erroneous reading, would be made.

This is a figure found under identically the same circumstances as the previously mentioned spirals; found along the lines of the Mayas and Carians running easterly from the Motherland. It is composed of the hieratic letter H or rather two of the letters following one another but connected with each other. The second is drawn in reverse of the first one, symbolizing a return.

These also are generally found at the entrance of burial chambers.

THE TREE AND THE SERPENT.—This work would seem incomplete to me if I omitted the Tree and the Serpent. Innumerable legends about the Serpent and the Tree are found in religions. The tree is invariably called "Tree of Life," and the serpent entwining it, "Tempter," or whatever else signifies Satan. The Tree and the Serpent started as a legend, then gradually drifted into myths: the climax being reached when the tree was credited with its fantastic crop of apples. These apples became necessary to carry out a myth for how otherwise could old Satan tempt Eve to eat apples and Eve tempt Adam? They were needed to accomplish the downfall of Adam. By this action poor woman has been made the cause of every ill befalling mankind. It is a monumental piece of cowardice on the part of man to put that responsibility on the shoulders of the woman. The irony is that a man and not a woman was to blame. The Eve alibi has stood for nearly 3,000 years but it must now be set aside. Had Ezra been able to read correctly the symbols which appeared in the writings of Moses, he would have given a very different version of the wily old Serpent and the Tree of Life (Plate V).

The small vignette comes from the Sacred Inspired Writings of Mu. These Sacred Writings teach that there *is only one real life on this earth,* which is the *Soul of Man,* and which these writings sometimes call *The Man* also *The Inner Man.* It was taught that man's material body was only a temporary habitation. All other forms which are known to us as life are of a temporary nature also. They are taken from the earth and to earth they must return. Of all the forms of earthly creations, man only had an imperishable part which survived the material body and lived on for ever; therefore *Man's Soul* was the only *true* life on earth.

Man *first* appeared on earth in the *Land of Mu;* therefore the *first actual life* on earth appeared in *Mu.* In these writings man is also spoken of as a fruit. Trees bear fruit, and man was the *first fruit* of a tree and the fruit was *life.* The Land of Mu was the Tree of Life. Thus Mu was symbolized as a tree—the Tree of Life.

In the vignette, the tree is shown as having a serpent coiled around it, thus *surrounding* the tree. It is an unadorned serpent, therefore it is Khan the symbol of Khanab, "The Great Waters," the ocean. Here it is symbolically shown that Mu was surrounded by water. Mu had no land connections with any other continental land. *The Serpent is the waters surrounding Mu.*

The foregoing shows and intelligently explains *what* the Tree of Life was, and *why* a Serpent is coiled around it. What Moses undoubtedly wrote were plain facts, in symbolical language—a symbolically written history, true in all respects. Translations, erroneous and misleading, perverted his writings.

THE ANCIENT MEANINGS OF CERTAIN NUMERALS. —The number 3 is now commonly called the lucky number. Why? We must go back to tradition to tell us.

I. The First Man, Dual Principle

Over 20,000 years old. From the ancient Uighur Capital,
beneath Karakhota, Gobi Desert.

II. The Hittite Bird Symbol

III. The Waters of the Mother of Life

IV. The Roadway of the Soul

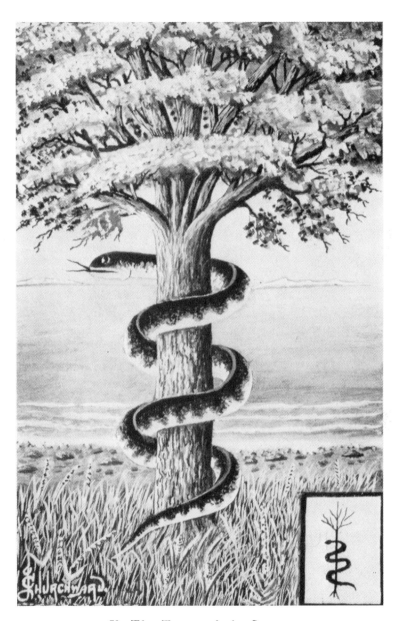

V. The Tree and the Serpent

VI. Vase of the Late Minoan I Period (about 1600–1500 B. C.) found on Gournia, Crete

VII. One of the two oldest known bronzes in the world. It is a symbolical figure of Mu as the mistress and ruler of the whole earth. It was made in either Mu or in the Uighur Capital City over 18,000 years ago.

On one occasion, I asked the old Rishi, "Do you know why we call the numeral three, the lucky number?" His answer was, "I can only surmise; what is three the symbol of?" My answer was, "Heaven and the Triune Godhead and, yes, the numeral symbol of the Motherland of Mu." He answered: "Don't you think man was lucky to have a Motherland, and more so to know that he will not meet the fate of the Motherland?"

He then turned and said to me: "Four is the lucky numeral because it is the Four Great Primary Forces that have charge of us and care for our material bodies through their earthly lives and their numeral is Four. In ancient times, Four stood amongst the most revered numbers, but today it is almost—if not entirely—forgotten. Possibly the mythical teachings of modern science has much to do with this loss. As Three is looked upon as the Lucky Number, Seven is looked upon as the Sacred Number."

THE SACRED SEVEN.—The original sacred *Seven* was the Seven Great Commands of the Creator. These were given to the Four Great Primary Forces, to carry out "his will, command or wishes," thus emanating from the Creator. They are the Creative Forces of the Almighty.

The predilection of ancient peoples in their sacred ceremonies for the use of the numeral Seven is very great and conspicuous.

Chaldeans: The Seven Days of rainfall that produced the "Flood."

Hindu: The Seven Days of the prophecy of the Flood made by Vishnu to Satyravata.

The Bible: The Seven Days of the prophecy of the Flood made by the Lord to Noah.

Babylonian: The Seven Vases used by the priests in their sacrifices.

Persian: The Seven Horses of the Aryans, that drew the chariot of the Sun. The Seven Apris or shapes of the flame. The Seven Rays of Agni.

Hindu: The Seven Steps of Buddha at his birth. The Seven Rishi Cities of India.

Egyptian: Their Seven Days of Creation. Their Seven Days of the week. And the Seven Classes of Egyptians.

Greek: The Seven Islands sacred to Proserpine. The Seven-headed Hydra killed by Hercules.

Norse: The Seven Families who accompanied the mythical Wotan, founder of the city of Nachan.

Hebrew: The Seven Lamps of the Ark. The Seven Branches of the Golden Candlestick. The Seven Days' Feast of the dedication. The Seven Years of plenty. And the Seven Years of famine. The Seven People who escaped from the flood.

Christians: The Seven Golden Candlesticks. The Seven Churches with the Seven Angels at their head. The Seven Heads of the beasts that rose from the sea. The Seven Seals of the Book. The Seven Trumpets of the angels. The Seven Vials of the wrath of God. The Seven Last Plagues of the Apocalypse.

Nahualts: The Seven Caves from which the ancestors of the Nahualts emerged.

Zuni Indians: The Seven Cities of Cibola.

Uighurs: The Seven Sacred cities of the Uighurs.

Atlantis: The Seven Great Cities of Atlantis.

Carian: The Seven Antilles.

Marquesan: The Seven People who were saved from the "Flood."

The Seven Marouts or genii of the winds in the hierarchy of Mazdeism.

The Seven Rounds of the ladder in the cave of Mirtha.

Mu, the Motherland: The Seven Sacred Cities with their golden gates.

The Hidden Meaning of One to Ten

English	Naga	Maya	The Hidden Meaning
1.	Hun.	Hun.	The Universal One
2.	Cas.	Ca.	The Dual God
3.	Ox.	Ox.	Who by His power caused
4.	San.	Can.	The Four Powerful Ones
5.	Ho.	Ho.	to come
6.	Uac.	Uac.	To arrange things in order
7.	Uuac.	Uuac.	to create, and
8.	Uaxax.	Uaxax.	to make man. To stand erect and
9.	Bolan.	Bolan.	to make his parts revolve on themselves
10.	Lahun.	Lahun.	He is two in one.

163

The Naga Form of Writing Numerals

1.	O	Hun
2.	OO	Cas.
3.	OOO	Ox.
4.	OOOO	Zan. (Hindu: *San*)
5.	▭	Ho
6.		Uac.
7.		Uuac.
8.		Uaxac.
9.		Bolan.
10.		Lahun.

The ancients counted in fives to avoid mentioning ten. Ten was the numeral of the Deity; therefore too sacred to be mentioned. Ten was counted twice five, fifteen three times five and so on up to twenty.

I will take one more example in numerals—the number 13. Thirteen is always looked upon as unlucky especially when in connection with Friday.

Mu, the Motherland, was destroyed on a Friday, the 13th day of the Month of Zac (the white month). The memory of that day, the 13th, has been carried down as an unlucky day for mankind.

CHAPTER VI

SYMBOLS RELATING TO MU

THE SACRED LOTUS.—The Lotus has always been looked upon as the most sacred of all sacred flowers—why? Because it was selected as Mu's floral symbol. Why was it so selected? The Lotus was the first flower to beautify the earth. Being the *first* flower and Mu the land where man *first* appeared on earth, Mu and the Lotus were naturally symbolic synonyms. As a mark of love and mourning, the Egyptians, after the destruction of Mu, never depicted the lotus as an open, living flower but always as closed and dead.

The lotus is a prominent figure in the carvings and adornments of all ancient temples, and, except in Egypt, was continued down as open and conventional until King Solomon's Temple. In this form, the tips of the petals are turned in.

The lotus was indigenous to Mu. The plant was carried to all parts of the world by the colonists, so that wherever we find the lotus today, we know that the parent stock, like the parent stock of man, came originally from Mu.

Fig. 2. The hieratic letter M in Mu's alphabet

165

Symbols relating to Mu

which was the alphabetical symbol for Mu as the Mother*land* of man.

Fig. 3. The second of the four glyphs for M in Mu's alphabet. This was the symbol for Mu as the *Mother* of man.

Fig. 4. This is the numeral 3. Three was the numeral symbol for Mu and very much used.

Fig. 5. The two lotus buds are the symbols for the two islands adjacent to Mu. Mu and these two islands were geologically known as the Lands of the West.

Fig. 6. An open lotus very much used in decorations and in traceries on temple walls, when it was desired to refer to Mu. The ends of the petals are turned in to denote Death.

Fig. 7. This is a symbol constantly appearing in the Maya writings and has been translated in every conceivable way except the correct one. Some of these decipherings are absolutely ludicrous, Le Plongeon's as an example. This glyph is a compound symbol being

composed of the second M in Mu's alphabet ⌐ , and

having at the end of each arm an imix ◉ the symbol

for breast. These breasts are shown distant from ⌐ the

mother; therefore physically not actually attached to it.

Cortez, as we are told by Bishop Landa, asked the natives what the symbol meant. Their answer was Mother. This is correct as far as it goes, but it does not

167

go far enough. ⌐ is the alphabetical symbol for Mu,

the mother of man. ⊕ These imix' say, the breast of
Mu. In many of the ancient writings the two islands
are called the breasts of Mu. Therefore a liberal translation would be "Mu, the Mother of Man," and because the two islands are included, the Lands of the
West. The imix is drawn as follows in the Troano
MS.:

Front view of the breast.

Representing side view of the breast.

Fig. 8. The withered and dying lotus: Mu's floral
symbol after she was dead.

Fig. 9. The Lands of the West, at the time she was
above water.

Fig. 10. Mu is submerged. No light shines upon
her. She is in the region of darkness.

Fig. 11. The Lands of the West are in darkness. No
light shines upon her.

Fig. 12. Mu, the Lands of the West. Maya.

Fig. 13. That Land of Kui—Maya writing.

Fig. 14. Peaks only remain above the watery abyss.
Codex Cortesianus.

Fig. 15. The ten tribes which were submerged with
Mu. Troano MS.

Fig. 16. Mu is sacrificed. She lies in the region of
darkness. Book of the Dead.

No. 4.

An Altar Painting

Fig. 17. The light of day has gone from Mu. Cliff writing, Nevada.

Fig. 18. Mu lies beyond the horizon over the great waters. Cliff writing, Nevada.

Fig. 19. The Tree and Serpent. Cliff writing, Nevada.

Fig. 20. The Tree and the Serpent, as it appears in the Sacred Writings.

Fig. 21. One of the forms of the letter M found in various ancient writings.

Fig. 22. The royal escutcheon of Mu.

Altar Painting—The Legend, Deciphering and Translation: This temple is dedicated to the Sacred Four—the Four Great Forces which issue from the mouth of The Almighty and are His commands. They first of all evolved law and order out of chaos throughout the Universe, and then created all things. They have now the charge of the physical welfare of all creations. They order and control the movements of the Universe today. This temple is under the jurisdiction of the mother church of Mu, whose High Priest is Ra Mu, who is the mouthpiece of the Almighty One.

This legend is a key to the extreme age of the Mexican tablets. The legend shows that at the time the temple was built Mu was above water, because the temple is under the jurisdiction of Mu. Mu was submerged about 10,000 B. C., thus showing that this temple was built *more* than *12,000 years ago,* but how much longer I have found nothing to indicate.

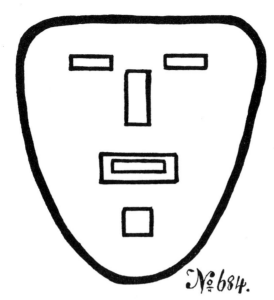

№ 684.

*"Mu, the Motherland, the Lands of
the West"*

№ 1055

*"The Lord God speaks through the mouth
of Mu"*

Mexican Tablet No. 684 reads: "Mu, the Motherland, the Lands of the West."

Mexican Tablet No. 1005 reads: "God speaks through the Mouth of Mu."

Legends on the Vignettes

"Mu, the Empire of the Sun, the Lands of the West, has fallen into an abyss. She is in the region of darkness, where the Sun never shines upon her. Her crown no longer rules the earth."

While there are scores, hundreds even, of writings that tell of the destruction of Mu, I have found only two tableaux depicting her destruction. First I found the Egyptian, and next this North American Indian. *Legend:* "The Creator considered the destruction of the Motherland of Man. So the Four Great Forces the executors of His commands caused the waters to swallow her up. They caused her to be carried down into a watery abyss and be submerged.

Three Vignettes from the Egyptian "Book of the Dead" depicting the destruction of Mu by falling into a "tank" of fire—a fiery pit. As she went down, flames arose around and enveloped her.

Fig. 1. No pillars showing.

Fig. 2. The Eastern pillar showing.

Thunder Bird and Whale

A North American Nootka Indian Tableau recounting the Submergence of Mu

Fig. 3. All of the four pillars are found showing.

This Egyptian Vignette shows one phase only of the destruction of Mu, how she sank into the fiery depths. The Nootka Indian shows the other phase, her burial by water. Arizona also supplies data on Mu's destruction by the symbolic pictures, pecked on her stones by the men of past ages. The American records are hoary with age.

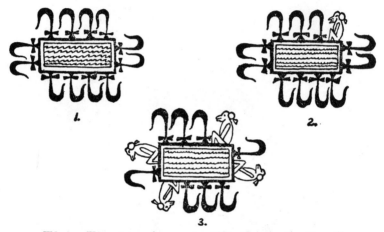

Three Vignettes from the "Book of the Dead"

A Mexican Stone Tablet: This is one of the most extraordinary tablets I have ever examined. It is a stone with highly glazed colors. The glyphs are like glass and have been cut out of the face of the stone—a fine sandstone—for a depth of about $\frac{1}{16}$th of an inch. The writings are in ancient, very ancient, characters used by the priesthood only. Of what age it is, I have no idea: but the one who arranged the glyphs had a temple knowledge. All of the glyphs are found among the

Tablet from Mexico
Destruction of Mu

Nagas only. It cannot be over 12,000 years old, because the writing is a description of the destruction of Mu. It was bought from an Indian in Mexico City who said he found it in a ruin. We must take the statement for what it is worth.

Legend: "Kuiland, The Great Ruler of the Earth, exists no longer. She was shaken up and down by earthquakes in various places. The land rolled like ocean swells. Finally, the Pillars that supported her gave way. She then sank into a fiery abyss. As the Great Ruler went down, flames from the fires of the underneath arose and enveloped her. The waters rolled in over her sunken form. Then was Kuiland, The Great Ruler, submerged."

The Field of Aarru, Chapter 110, "Book of the Dead." This large vignette, one of the largest in the the Book of the Dead, was not comprehended by Ezra or any of his associates. Neither has it been comprehended by any Egyptologist of the present time. To substantiate my contention I have shown the two ends of this symbolic picture.

The Vignette depicts the life of man in the Motherland. The lower part is a conventional map of Mu. On the left hand top corner of the upper part, there are three cartouches bearing the names of three waters, shown in the lower part. The lower part also shows three lands, each surrounded by water. The names of these waters as read by Egyptologists are: Power of waters. Innumerable waters. Great place of waters.

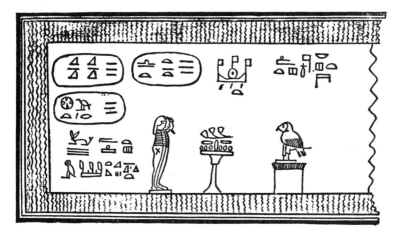

The beginning of the Vignette

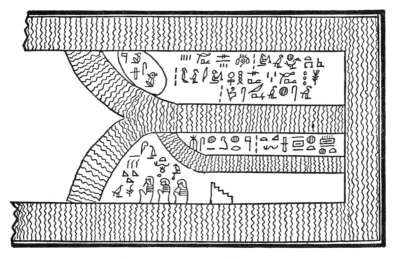

The end of the Vignette
The Field of Aarru, Chapter 110, "Book of the Dead"

Now let us see what Ezra's translations of them are: Genesis, Chapter 2, Verse 11. "The name of the first is Pison. The name of the second Gihon. And the third Hiddekel." Next I shall take the Biblical boundaries of the Garden of Eden. They are given thus:—

Verse 8 And the Lord God planted a garden *eastward* in Eden and there he put the man whom he had formed.

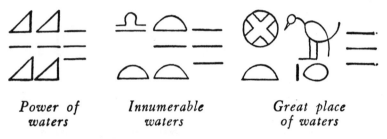

| Power of waters | Innumerable waters | Great place of waters |

(Anyone looking at the map today taking in Ethiopia, Assyria and the Valley of the Euphrates—and seeing how a land might possibly cover this area—to represent either an island or a garden, must at once feel that the Biblical description is purely symbolical, which is corroborated in Verse 8, where it says the garden was *eastward* in Eden. Where this was written was either in Egypt or Palestine—therefore, according to present general acceptance, in the middle of the garden itself, being in the east or towards the east is a link showing the Garden of Eden that was Mu in another vestment.)

Verse 9 And out of the ground made the Lord God to grow every tree that is pleasant to the sight, and good for food: the tree of life also in the midst of the garden, and the tree of knowledge of good and evil.

Verse 10 And a river went out of Eden to water the garden; and from thence it was parted, and became into four heads.

Verse 11 The name of the first is Pison, that is it which compassed the whole land of Havilah, where there is gold.

Verse 12 And the gold of that land is good, there is bedellium and the onyx stone.

Verse 13 And the name of the second river is Gihon the same it is that compasseth the whole land of Ethiopia.

Verse 14 And the name of the third river is Hiddekel: that is it which goeth towards the east of Assyria, and the fourth river is Euphrates.

The Four Genii, as I have previously stated, were, to my mind another vestment of the Sacred Four; which, in turn were given the name of the Four Great Pillars, the executors of the Creator's commands.

The Genii appeared to be very popular among all ancient peoples since the demise of Mu for I do not find their names before that date. But in all nations and peoples during the past 10,000 or 11,000 years the Genii are quite prominent. Most of the ancient peoples seem to have had a varied conception of them, and how they should be described. I find them associated with all histories and traditions of the creation. One of the oldest records that I have found of them comes from the

Mayas of Yucatan and Central America. With them the Genii were referred to as "the Keepers of the Pillars."

The Mayas as well as all other ancients symbolized the earth as a four-sided square. At times and for certain purposes, for explanation, they stood the square on one of its points forming a diamond out of it. This brought the four points into astronomical lines pointing north, south, east and west, making Four Cardinal Points. The theology said—that at these four points, were four pillars sustaining heaven, and at the foot of each pillar, was stationed one of the Genii, to look after and care for it. The names of the Maya genii were:—

Kan-Bacab—the Yellow Bacab, placed in the South.
Chac-Bacab—the Red Bacab, placed in the East.
Zac-Bacab—the White Bacab, placed in the North.
Ec-Bacab—the Black Bacab, placed in the West.
It is thus seen that the Mayas, chose to define their genii by colors.

The Hindus had four Genii presiding at their Four Cardinal Points. (The Hindus used the words cardinal points symbolically. They did not refer to any particular spot or spots, but to wherever they might be.)

Instead of colors their Genii were called by phenomena connected with life, their names were:—

Rouvera—the God of Wealth, placed in the North.
Yama—the Judge of the Dead, placed in the South.
Indra—the King of Heaven, placed in the East.
Varona—the God of the Waters, placed in the West.
The Genii were also called gods by the Hindus.

Chinese. The Chinese designated their Genii as Yo's —mountains. The four mountains Tse-Yo. They also referred to them as the four quarters of the earth. They are

Tai-Tsong—the Yo of the East.

Saing-Fou—the Yo of the West.

How-Kowang—the Yo of the South.

Chin-Si—the Yo of the North.

The Chinese symbolized these mountains as a mountain in the shape of a triangle with an eye at the apex of the mountain looking down from it.

Egyptian. According to the Egyptian theology there were Four Genii in Amenti, which were placed at the Four Cardinal Points in charge of the pillar which stood there, their names were:—

Amset—the genius at the Cardinal Point in the East.

Hapu—the genius at the Cardinal Point in the West.

Tesautmutf—the genius at the Cardinal Point in the North.

Quabsenuf—the genius at the Cardinal Point in the South.

Chap. 125, Book of the Dead, has a large picture of the great Hall of Truth of Osiris. Near the seat of Osiris in this picture are shown the Four Genii. They are symbolized as men in mummy form. One has the head of a human being, another the head of a monkey, a third the head of a hawk, and the fourth the head of a jackal (Anubis).

Chaldean. The Chaldeans believed that there were

Four Genii protecting and looking after the welfare of all human beings. This example does much to show the origin of the genii. As by the swastika, we frequently see in the ancient writings that man's welfare is constantly being watched over by the Sacred Four, symbolized by crosses et cetera, and that by watching over and caring for the physical welfare of the universe, including man, they are acting as the executors of the Creator's wishes, desires, commandments et cetera. This is the exact work of the genii as conceived by the Chaldeans. The names given to the genii by the Chaldeans are:—

Sed-Alap or *Kirub*—Represented as a bull with a human face.

Lamas or *Nigal*—Represented as a lion with a man's head.

Ustar—After the human likeness.

Nattig—Represented with the head of an eagle.

The Hittites, Assyrians and *Persians* all had the Genii engrafted in their cosmogony.

The Israelites. Although I cannot find any direct reference in the Jewish research which I have made, that is no criterion and does not say that they entirely rejected the idea.

In Ezekiel, Chapter I, Verse 10, there is something at least touching on it, for it says: "They four had the face of a man, and the face of a lion, on the right side: and they four had the face of an ox on the left side; they four also had the face of an eagle." The foregoing is given as a vision of Ezekiel. At the time this was written Ezekiel was a captive among the Chaldeans.

Let us compare this vision with the Chaldean creed which had been in existence thousands of years before Ezekiel came on earth.

Ezekiel's dream. Four beasts with the heads of a man, another an ox, another a lion, and the fourth, an eagle.

Chaldean Belief. Four Genii, beasts with heads; one with a human face, one with a face of a bull one with the face of a lion and the fourth with the face of an eagle. These Chaldean genii stood at the bottom of steps leading to temples and palaces, one could not walk through a city without seeing many of them.

Thus to me it seems unquestionable that Ezekiel must have seen many of them during his captivity. A set of four is now in the British Museum and came from the king's palace, Nineveh. Ezekiel's vision looks like an embellishment of the Chaldean Creed. Is the Biblical translation correct?

HIERATIC LETTERS FROM THE ALPHABET OF MU

The hieratic letter A, pronounced Ahau. The monotheistic alphabetical symbol of the Deity.

The hieratic letter H, the alphabetical symbol of the Four Great Primary Forces, called in the Sacred Inspired Writings, "the Sacred Four."

The hieratic letter M, pronounced Mā and Mu, the *u* is pronounced as in German u. The alphabetical

symbol of Mu, the Motherland. It was also the symbol for mother, earth, land, country, empire, anything pertaining to the soil.

The hieratic letter N, the alphabetical symbol for the Serpent of Creation.

The hieratic letter T, pronounced Tāó, the alphabetical symbol for resurrection, also emersion. Used in the Sacred Writings symbolizing Mu's emersion.

The hieratic letter U, pronounced as *oo* in moon. The alphabetical symbol for an abyss, a deep hole, a valley. In the body of a word another of the "u" glyphs is generally used as a V.

Dress ornament
Society Islands

Dress ornament
Marquesan

THE SACRED SYMBOLS OF MU

SOME MISCELLANEOUS SYMBOLS RELATING TO MU

This glyph is often found in ancient writings. It is one of the figures that was used to symbolize the Four Great Primary Forces—the Sacred Four. It is composed of four circles, each with one of its sides incomplete.

Another glyph symbolizing the Sacred Four. This was a very favorite symbol among the Uighurs and is revered by the Chinese today. I have also found it as a dress ornamentation among the South Sea Islanders especially the Polynesians.

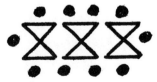

This peculiar glyph is found in various parts of the earth, but not often. I have found it in writings where

186

the ten tribes of people who went down with the Motherland at her destruction are spoken of.

Apparently this is a Maya symbol. I have found it in no other writings. It is found in the Maya description of the destruction of the Motherland. It reads: "Peaks only rise out of the abyss." It therefore refers to the islands that were formed between the gas chambers.

An equilateral triangle with the monotheistic symbol of the Deity within symbolizes: the triangle—Heaven, The circle within—the Deity, reading the Deity, the Infinite, dwells in Heaven, Heaven is His abode.

An equilateral triangle with an eye within symbolizes the Deity looking out from heaven. In Egypt it was changed to the all seeing Eye of Osiris looking down from heaven. These two symbols are found in all ancient writings. Rather, they appear in many writings and among all people.

A large dot within a small circle was occasionally

used by the Egyptians as an equivalent for an eye.

A conventional map of the Lands of the West after submersion. (From the Troano Manuscript.)

CHAPTER VII

SACRED SYMBOLS CONNECTING NORTH AMERICA TO MU

SLABS FROM PATAMBO.—These two slabs were found by William Niven in an ancient grave on the banks of the river Rio del Oro in the state of Guerraro, Mexico. They are not the work of a very ancient civilization like those of Chimalpa, Remedios et cetera. This civilization occupied Mexico *less* than 12,000 years ago as is shown by the inscription on one of the tablets, "returned to the region of darkness" which was *submerged* Mu.

Their actual age I cannot estimate. Each slab has a top and bottom division. The divisions are formed by a carved line running horizontally across the face of the slab near its center. The central figure in each of the top divisions is a conventional, symbolical head of Quetzalcoatl the bearded or feathered serpent, the symbolic serpent of the Creator in one part of Mu, and corresponds with Naga or Narayana the seven-headed serpent of Oriental countries.

The ancient peoples of North America had various names for their Serpent of Creation. The Quiches called it Gucumatz, the serpent covered with feathers.

Sculptured Slab A.

Found by William Niven in a grave at Rio del Oro near Placeres del Oro, state of Guerrero, Mexico. Size—28 inches long, 18 inches wide and 2 inches thick.

The Mayas called it Ac le Chapat, the plumed or feathered serpent. The Quetzals, the first of men who trod the soil of America called it Quetzalcoatl, the bearded serpent.

The Pueblo Indians of Arizona and New Mexico, even at the present time, call it Quetzalcoatl, the bearded serpent, thus showing that many thousands of years ago there was an intimate religious connection between the Pueblo Indians and this past civilization which dwelt in the valley of Rio del Oro, Mexico. An interesting question arises. Were they intimately connected by blood? Or were they even the same people? The Quetzals, the first people to arrive in America, took their name from this serpent in the Motherland just as the Oriental Nagas took their name from Naga, their serpent of creation.

These two slabs have far reaching significance. They are filled with hieratic letters from the alphabet of Mu. I can find nothing on these slabs to even intimate by what name these people were known.

Slab A. Upper Division. The central figure of the upper division of this slab consists of portions of the head of a symbolical serpent called Quetzalcoatl, the bearded, also the feathered serpent. A very important detail in the head are the eyes. This part of the carving is too mutilated to make anything out of it. The *beard* of the serpent is prominent and intact; this alone is sufficient to say to what serpent it belongs.

The mouth is an oblong square in the form of the hieratic letter M.

Evidently the nose and eyebrows are formed by a pair of serpents in the act of gliding away, leaving for some reason.

The head is resting on the hieratic letter U, the symbol of an abyss, deep down, et cetera.

The ends of the U are bent outwards ending with the symbol of the sun as *Kin,* not Ra, thus showing that it is the earth referred to and not heaven. The bottom part of this division assumes the form of an urn, symbolizing the body of the earth. The U opening at the top symbolizes the abyss. Within this urn are two glyphs, squares pointing downward with the symbol, "lost light," engraved upon them (literal translation— The light has gone forth from the day).

Slab A. Lower Division. This division symbolizes a grave where the body is lying in rest and darkness as shown by the pointer glyphs. In the upper division the pointer indicated downward, the direction taken by the body. Here the pointer is changed to horizontal.

The design of this lower division is the two halves of a head placed back to back with each other. The eyes are again formed of the sun as Kin, the celestial orb, again telling us that this tableau refers to the earth, not to heaven.

Beneath the eyes are two conventional mouths in the form of the hieratic letter M. This form of M was used both by the Mayas and Egyptians.

Within these mouths is another hieratic letter, the letter N, which was the alphabetical symbol of the Serpent of Creation. This symbol is universal throughout the ancient world.

The American Serpent of Creation is adorned with either feathers or a beard, the Oriental with seven heads, but in all cases, wherever found, an adorned serpent is the symbol of the Creator and Creation and among all ancient peoples the hieratic letter N was its alphabetical symbol. Thus we find here in America, the same symbol used as in the Orient.

Slab A. The Legend. Quetzalcoatl, the Creator, the Bearded Serpent called him, and his soul passed on to the region of darkness (submerged Mu) there to await the call from the great serpent for re-incarnation.

Slab. B. Slab B, like Slab A, has two divisions, an upper and a lower. These two slabs are so intimately connected that they may be looked upon as belonging to the same legend—Life and Death. Slab A symbolized Death and B, Life.

Upper Division. The central figure in this tableau is also the conventional head of the Bearded Serpent, Quetzalcoatl. In this drawing the action of the two serpents forming the nose and eyebrows differ from that in Slab A. Instead of gliding away, they are here shown with their heads bent towards the eyes. The double tongue of the serpents is curving around the eye, not striking it. Their tongues form the symbol for speech, so they are giving a command.

Sculptured Slab B.

Above and surrounding the head is the hieratic diphthong letter, Dz, a glyph with three steps, which symbolizes the three steps to the throne.

In the right hand lower corner of the slab the margin forms another Dz with the addition Am. It now reads Dzam, translated—He who sits upon the throne. At the foot of the throne is the monotheistic symbol of the Creator. Consequently, it is He, the Creator, who sits upon the throne.

The head, as in Slab A, rests over an urn having also an opening at the top in the form of U. This urn has an ornamental border composed of a string or succession of the hieratic letter N. This appears to me to form a strong adjective. Within the body of the urn which symbolizes the body of the earth are two glyphs, symbolizing darkness, i. e. the region of darkness, submerged Mu.

Lower Division. In the lower division of Slab B we find the exact opposite of Slab A. Here we find the two halves of the head brought together again and joined with opened, light-seeing eyes. This symbolizes the soul and body being joined together again, the re-incarnation. This face is twice repeated, the second forming the adjective to the accomplishment. The mouth in both faces is the oblong square, the symbol of Mu, thus saying that it is in Mu that the re-incarnation has taken place.

This is identically the same conception as the Egyptian where the soul returns to "Amenti," "The region of darkness," "The domain of Osiris," "Submerged Mu." It was also the conception of the Mayas of Yucatan, as it is in some Oriental countries today.

On each side of the lower division there are symbolical borders. The border on the left is composed of the third glyph of the letter H in Mu's alphabet and extends from the top to the bottom of the division. On the right hand border at the top is the hieratic letter H, the symbol of the Sacred Four.

The various symbols on the right hand border read: "the great serpent, who created all things. He who sits upon the throne. He who embodies the Sacred Four."

The Legend. When Quetzalcoatl, the Bearded Serpent, the Creator, he who sits upon the throne, whose Four Great Commands evolved law and order out of chaos, calls—the eyes of those closed in sleep are opened, the time of their re-incarnation has arrived. They answer the call of the Great Serpent and come forth into a new day.

Note. The glyphs on these slabs show an intimate connection between these people and the ancient Mayas of Yucatan. They were also closely connected with the people of Arizona and New Mexico. The cosmogony of all three is identical.

QUETZAL AND QUETZACOATL.—A popular misconception is that the sun was worshipped by the ancients. A parallel misconception exists about Quetzal and Quetzalcoatl.

Quetzals was the name of the first people whose feet

trod the soil of America, who were a blond race with
light flaxen hair. Their last king was called Quetzal.
They derived their name Quetzals from their chief
symbol for the commands of the Creator, the serpent,
Quetzalcoatl.

Quetzalcoatl is a feathered and *winged* serpent. In
the Motherland to the South of the Quetzals were a
people whose corresponding symbol was the Cobra-de-
Capella, which they called Naga. They were known as
the Nagas. They gave their Naga seven heads to correspond with the Seven Commands" or mental planes
of creation. The early settlers in North America, coming, generally, from the northern parts of the Motherland, made the feathered serpent their symbol.

In the ancient Quiche Maya sacred book, the *Popol
Vuh,* which was written in Guatemala, the Quetzalcoatl
is referred to as "the serpent covered with feathers" and
the symbol of Creation.

In Guatemala, where the Popol Vuh was written,
legends permeate the country, in which Quetzal is referred to as "the last king of the blond white race"
which occupied Central America and Southern
Mexico.

Among the Mayas of Yucatan of later date I find
that two different serpents were used to symbolize the
creative commands: the Naga, the seven-headed serpent
which they called Ac-la-Chapat, and the Quetzalcoatl,
which they called kukul-khan. Kukul comes out of two
words of the language of Mu, kuk—a feather and ul—

covered with, coated with et cetera, a free reading is, "covered with feathers."

The Aztecs as usual made a scramble out of the two words Quetzal and Quetzalcoatl, and after being thoroughly scrambled they turned the pan over, and out came Quetzalcoatl as the god. Then to add to the mix-up they gave this serpent-man, or god, a son, which they called Tescat, who was to be an avenger, for having taken the land from the Quetzals and driven them out of the country.

With this combination the Aztec priesthood instilled terror into the hearts of the people throughout the land. Their teachings were that the only way to appease Tescat was by human sacrifices. Thus human sacrifices were introduced by this vile priesthood, rivers of blood flowed throughout the land.

All people, even the king, lived in dread of the priesthood for no one knew but that he or she might be the next to be stretched upon the bloody stone. Thus the priesthood gained their point. They held control of life and property throughout the land.

In an old Spanish book written about the time of Cortez it says that: "when Cortez invaded Mexico more than 50,000 human sacrifices were carried out annually." As these old Spanish writers were not very accurate about what they wrote this passage of theirs should be discounted. It might have been more or it might have been less. All one can say is an immense number were sacrificed.

The Oriental Dragon is only a conventional Quetzal-coatl. I find that when either Naga or Quetzalcoatl is shown by any and *all* ancient peoples it is invariably in some conventional form. The forms of Quetzalcoatl are, none of them, anything like the serpent itself, except in being feathered.

The dragon is probably the most grotesque of all. Among the North American Indians I have never found the Naga, and only a few of the tribes have the feathered or plumed serpent, so far as I have yet learned.

Is Quetzalcoatl a mythical serpent? No, it is not. Quetzalcoatl is a feathered flying serpent, and the most venomous ever recorded: for, within two minutes, and apparently almost suddenly, the victim falls to the ground dead after being struck. The reptile is of a very peculiar shape, having a body about the size of a duck or small goose. The real serpent part of it is its head and neck, which, in the one I refer to extended about five feet from the body. The head is very broad, flat and V shaped, like most of our known venomous serpents. Apparently it had no snake-like tail, but in its place a tuft of short feathers. From the head to the body the neck is covered with short hair-like feathers. The general color of the neck and body is almost white, thickly mottled with grey; the upper wing feathers are very long and droop like the bird of paradise. These have a prismatic sheen. Their flight is very clumsy, and then they can only fly a very short distance, a few yards. Apparently they have great difficulty in settling on the branch of a tree. A soft-nosed bullet from a 30-30 so mashed and cut the one referred to that it is pretty difficult to describe it accurately. The meeting of this reptile ended in a triple tragedy. The Indians would go no farther, so the explorer returned.

It is said by the Indians that the Quetzalcoatl is to be *occasionally* found back in the swampy deep unexplored forests of Yucatan and Guatamala, but is very scarce.

Niven's Mexican tablets show that over 12,000 years ago Quetzalcoatl was used as a symbol by the people who occupied the Valley of Mexico at that time.

THE ORIGIN OF THE RED INDIAN.—I will now make a short review of the North American Indians, showing that nearly, if not all of our Red Indian Brothers, have among themselves vast numbers of Mu's original Sacred Symbols, retaining almost identically the same meanings they conveyed in Mu. These supplemented with their astounding legends show us clearly that the North American Indians came to America from Mu in *boats.*

Times without number, it has been scientifically recorded that the North American Indians came to America from Asia via the old Bering Land Bridge. They neither came from Asia nor did they use the Bering Land Bridge, and from their own legends and writings I shall show from where they actually came and how they came to America.

The trouble with our scientists in the past has been that when they came across anything they could neither comprehend nor understand, they cordially agreed that "It came from Asia via the Bering Land Bridge." Being thus agreed, it became orthodox science.

Our American scientists were not alone in piling up scientific accusations against Asia. The European scientists have splendidly seconded their American cousins in this respect. But the Europeans had no dear old bridge to carry their woes, so they dumped them on the Caucasian plains, the boundary line between Eastern Europe and Asia, saying: "It came from somewhere in the mountains of Central Asia." Then this became orthodox science. The Caucasian Plain myth like the Bering Land Bridge dream has broken up. The European scientists have turned their venom on Africa, and are accusing it of the most unheard of things. That is no business of ours, we have our own troubles to account for our Red-Skin Brothers. We cannot deny that they are here, and that they were here when we first came to America to make it our home; so they must originally have come from somewhere, but where? I am going to commence with the Indians down in Arizona and New Mexico, then work my way up through our Western States to British Columbia and Alaska. My keystone will be—two Indian *writings, not legends, written by the Indians themselves.* These writings tell us of their origin and where they came from to America, *also,* how they came.

In Arizona, New Mexico, Colorado, Nevada, Utah, et cetera, are various tribes of Pueblo Indians. They have many legends and traditions about their ancient past. During the short time I spent among them in Arizona and New Mexico they told me many of their legends. At a ceremonial dance I was astonished to see that the blanket of the Chief was covered with the Sacred Symbols of the Motherland, Mu. One symbol in particular attracted my attention, as it was identically like the central figure of the Hindu Cosmic Diagram, the Sri Santara. It is also the same as the Motherland's, with one exception. In the Motherland's Diagram the Twelve Gates to the World Beyond, are symbolized by twelve scallops. The Pueblos like the Hindus have symbolized theirs by twelve triangle points.

It is needless to say that when I read the symbols which appeared on the Chief's blanket, and told them their meanings, which were what they understood themselves, it was the open sesame for me to their hearts. I became at once a brother.

They have a legend, "That far, far back, they did not live in America, but in a land in the direction of the setting Sun, across the great waters. That their forefathers came from this land to America in boats."

They have a very complicated legend about the great flood. It varies a great deal in minor details by different narrators, but in all essential points it is the same.

Many of their present day words are to be found in Mu's vocabulary. Also, many of their other words have their roots in words of the Mother tongue.

Certain symbols persist from the north of Yucatan in

Mexico to Nevada, Utah and Colorado, which leads one to believe that at one time all this area was occupied by Pueblos or near relatives.

Having come to America from the Motherland in boats it shows that the Pueblos have been in America more than 12,000 years, the approximate date of Mu's destruction.

When they came to America they were a very highly educated, civilized people. Their legends show that they knew more about geology than our scientists did fifty years ago.

Why do we find them in the state they are today? The answer is the old, old, tale of mountain raising. When the mountains were raised, the earth went through a period of volcanic upheavals and workings such as she had never known before nor since. The outside parts of the earth's crust were literally torn to pieces. They were then forced up into ridges by the volcanic gases beneath; rocks were hurled and thrown from ridge to ridge, covering the valleys between. The earthquakes shook all cities and buildings into ruins, burying tens of millions of human beings in the débris.

Then to complete the destruction, the most violent volcanic outbursts followed. Fire, rocks, lava and smoke were belched forth burying the whole of the surrounding country with these ejections. Few of the people in the regions of the rising mountains escaped with their lives, a few here and there only.

An Oriental legend states that nearly a billion of

NEVADA.

lives were lost in Asia during the raising of the Asiatic mountains. In America stands a lava flow twenty-six feet thick and nearly thirty miles long. This is from one out of many surrounding craters. I find no record of the loss of life in America, it was, however, great.

After the mountains went up destroying most of the people and their country, the surviving Pueblos, to carry on, had to resort to primitive methods, so that they could only carry down by legends a few details of their great past.

Nevada. The following symbols have been found carved upon the rocks of Nevada. Some of them were etched before the mountains were raised on which they now stand, others were written after the mountains had gone up. There are two distinct dates when these writings were made. Those that were etched after the mountains went up are much more recent than those which were written before the mountains were raised. Probably thousands of years intervened between the two.

Among these Nevada writings there are three very distinct sets.

1. This is a symbol of the rising sun. Universal throughout the world.

2. Symbol of the setting sun. Universal throughout the world.

3. Symbol of the sun at his meridian. Universal throughout the world.

4. Symbol of the Sacred Four. The Four Great

THE SACRED SYMBOLS OF MU

Primary Forces. Universal throughout the world.

5. Symbol of the sun as Ra. Universal throughout the world. This is the earliest pattern of the Sun as Ra.

6. The plain colored disk without rays symbolizes that the sun has sunk below the horizon and is giving no light to the land.

7. A colored disk with three feathers appearing above symbolizes: First the plain disk—darkness—Second the three feathers symbolizes Mu— A free reading— Mu is in the region of darkness, no light shines upon her, she is dead, submerged.

8. This an open cross within a circle and reads U luumil Kin. The land of the sun. The empire of the sun. The sun is here called Kin, not Ra. Kin was the name of the sun as the celestial orb, not the symbol. Note the difference in the two crosses No. 4 and this. No. 4 is a solid cross and this is an open one.

9. The hieratic letter A, Naga pattern symbolizing the great ruler, the Creator, the Deity.

10. This is another symbol of the Sacred Four, one of the steps towards the swastika in its evolution. This symbol superseded No. 4. It is now two steps from the swastika.

11. This is a little vignette saying that Mu lies beyond the horizon across the great water. The serpent is Khan the great water. The Arc is the symbol of the horizon and the three feathers is one of Mu's symbols. Her numeral symbol—three.

12. I am unable to give this.

13. This is an inscription reading Chi-po-ze, which translated reads: "A mouth opened, fires came forth with vapours, the pillars gave way, the land went down."

14. A serpent unadorned, the symbol for water. This might have been a guide post pointing the way to water.

15. One of the glyphs of the letter H in the Motherland's alphabet.

16. This symbol was called by the ancients the Mysterious Writing. Its import is the same as the Cardinal number 1.

17. The tree and the Serpent. I have given the origin and meaning of this.

18. This reads: The great ruler—The empire of the sun.

19. This symbolizes the contour of some land with two islands adjacent.

20. This glyph is the Life Symbol. It appears hundreds of times in the Egyptian Book of the Dead. An exact duplication of this glyph will be found at the base of the Naos or Chair of Osiris. There it is many times repeated. Book of the Dead, Chapter 125.

21. This is the bud of a lotus flower. The floral symbol of Mu. The sacred flower among all ancient peoples.

22. An Uighur Symbol. Gone down from the sight of the sun.

23. An Uighur symbol, Mehen—Man.

24. The original symbol for the Sacred Four. Found

in the Sacred Inspired Writings of Mu. This symbol was universal throughout the world.

25. The ancient symbol for water. Universal throughout the world.

26. The hieratic letter U. Symbol for an abyss, a deep hole, a valley. Universal throughout the world.

27. This is a guide telling the way to a temple which is dedicated to the Sacred Four.

28. An Uighur symbol. I cannot give the meaning.

29. An Uighur symbol, the letter X.

30. An Uighur symbol for hard.

31. An Uighur symbol, heaven above earth.

32. An Uighur pattern of the feather, symbol for Truth. Universal throughout the world.

33. One of the glyphs for the letter N in the alphabet of the Motherland.

34. A human hand, not a symbol.

35. The ancient symbol for the active and passive elements in nature. Universal throughout the world.

36. An Uighur symbol, fires of the underneath.

37. An Uighur pattern of the symbol for multitudes. The Egyptians reversed the leaf, having the stem on top.

38. An outline of an animal, not a symbol.

39. The skin of an animal, not a symbol.

40. Tracks of an animal, not a symbol.

41. An animal's head, not a symbol.

42. One of the glyphs of the letter H in the alphabet of the Motherland.

SACRED SYMBOLS

A. B. C. D. E. are symbols perfectly new to me. I have no key whereby I can read them: and there are not enough out of which to form a key.

In this collection of Nevada symbols, there is a great mix-up of Naga and Uighur characters. They show, however, a very close connection with the ancients of both Yucatan and the people who wrote Niven's Stone tablets.

There are two distinct eras of writings, written by neither Naga, Uighur nor Yucatan Maya, probably one or two of the ten tribes of the Motherland, who were in close proximity with all three in the Motherland.

Among the Klamath Indians of Oregon there are to be found several legends—one about a great flood. In Washington and British Columbia among the Kooteney Indians they have a legend stating that, "their forefathers came to America from the Land of the Sun." Land of the Sun and Empire of the Sun were the common names for Mu before she was submerged.

Upon one of their ceremonial dresses I found a border with the hieratic letter M, Mu's alphabetical symbol. Prominently resting over the left breast of the wearer was an emblem, an eight-rayed Sun, the central figure of Mu's escutcheon.

The Sun was a pale yellow, the rays of a warm pinkish red with their points a pale blue. Blue was Mu's symbolic color.

I think this symbol in conjunction with their legend clearly proves that the forefathers of the Kooteney

Ornament on a ceremonial blanket
Koteney Indian, British Columbia

Fan with Mu's symbol, eight
pointed sun
Gilbert Islands

Indians originally came from Mu; also that they themselves are aware of the fact.

I will now take a leaf out of the history of the Haiden Indians of Queen Charlotte Island, near Alaska. The leaf is a totem pole, one of the prettiest and one of the most interesting totem poles I have ever seen. The pole is capped with a large eagle-like looking bird which is called the *Thunder Bird*. Extending nearly the whole length of the pole is a symbolical fish which is called the *Killer Whale*. About half-way between the head and tail of the fish stands a man who is thrusting a spear into the back of the fish. This man is called the *Steelheaded Man*.

A very wise, wizened old Chief, who thoroughly understood the legends of his people, kindly explained the symbols on the pole as follows: "The winged creature that crowns the pole is the *Thunder Bird—representative of the Creator*.

"Lightning is the winking of the Thunder Bird's sharp eyes, and thunder is the flapping of its wings. Rain is the spilling of water from a huge lake in the middle of its immense back. The talons of the bird are fastened in the tail of the Killer Whale."

This is all symbolical; let us see what it all means. First the bird is a representative of the Creator. From other ancient writings this statement is elucidated by saying the Bird symbolizes the Forces which carried out the commands of the Creator— His executors in creation. Birds as symbols for the Creative Forces are common throughout the world. The Thunder Bird appears to be the universal symbol among the Indians of our Northwest. Thunder, lightning, rain, et cetera, are ascribed to the Thunder Bird. This is again true, the Thunder Bird being the executive of the Supreme Power. The natural phenomena result from the workings of what we call nature, and nature is the will of the Supreme. Bird Symbols for the Four Great Creative Forces are found in Mexico, Central America, Egypt, Assyria, Babylonia, India, among the Hittites, et cetera, in fact among all ancient people, so that the Thunder Bird follows in line with the rest.

The Killer Whale is the symbol for ocean waters among the North American Indians of our Northwest. Most of the ancients used an unadorned serpent to symbolize the waters which they called Khanab. The name Killer Whale was probably given to it, on account of its drowning the 64,000,000 millions of people when the Motherland Mu was submerged.

The Steeled-headed Man. I will now resume the old Chief's description— "The man piercing the back of the Killer Whale is the Steel-headed Man. In the days of the great flood *the Steel-headed man was the leader of all men,* and much beloved by the Thunder Bird, the Thunder God and all other gods. When the flood swept over the face of the earth the gods feared for the life of the Steeled-headed man whom they miraculously changed into a Steeled-headed salmon."

There again we have a great symbolism. It says the

Steel-headed man was the leader or governor of all men. This clinches the point that the Steel-headed man was the symbol of Mu among the Haiden Indians. Ancient literature is permeated with sayings that "Mu was the ruler of all mankind," "Mu rules the earth," and in the Maya book, the Codex Cortesianus, Mu is referred to as "The Great Ruler," "The Great Ruler exists no longer," et cetera.

I will again return to the Chief's description: "During the days of the flood, the transformed leader of men lived in the waters of the Minkish River. He gathered the posts and timber for his dwelling, but found he lacked strength to do the building. Then the Thunder Bird appeared before the Steel-headed man in a crashing and rumbling of Thunder. The Thunder Bird lifted his god mask and revealed a human face to the Steel-headed man, 'I am as human as you' said the bird, 'and I will put up the timbers for you. There shall I stay with you to set up your tribe and be your protector for ever.' Then with four claps of thunder, the bird caused to appear a group of warriors who sprang out of the crashing din full armed. They with the Steel-headed man were the nucleus from which the Haiden people grew."

There we have a myth so covering a legend that it becomes hard to extract the legend from the myth.

Steel and Steel-headed Salmon were names unknown in America, up to a few hundred years ago.

At this point there is also an omission in the legend.

How did the Steel-headed Salmon become a man again? How did the group of warriors arrive, and where did they come from? There is no mention of women without whom the tribe could not be formed.

In many of the Oriental pictures of emigrants leaving Mu by boat, they are pictured as fish jumping along on the surface of the water. Was the Steel-headed man one of these jumping fishes?

In completing the reading of the totem pole the old Chief said that the base told the tale of:

The Killer Whale and the Sea Lion. "The Sea Lion was helping a warrior to save his wife from the Killer Whale (drowning) when he was overcome and struck down by the Killer Whale (the waters). He was saved and restored to his family by Kolus the protecting god of the household. The Sea Lion was made a member of the tribe and married the warrior princess, the daughter of the Steel-headed man." The Sea Lion was unquestionably a man of another tribe whose totem was the Sea Lion. In ancient times it was usual to call a man by the name of his totem.

One of the most extraordinary picture writings I have ever come across is a painted tableau depicting the submersion of Mu, and one of two pictures only that I have found depicting the submersion of Mu. The other is the Egyptian. The picture has three archaeological divisions:—*Top*—A serpent with a plume of feathers on its head. *Middle*—The Thunder Bird with its talons embedded in the body of the Killer Whale. *Bottom*

—The Killer Whale covered with symbols. This tableau comes from the Nootka Indians who live on the west coast of Vancouver Island, British Columbia, Canada.

While there are hundreds of writings telling of the destruction of Mu, also various compound symbols forming vignettes in the ancient Maya writings, throughout the world I have only found two tableaux or pictures showing the manner of her destruction, the Egyptian and now the Nootka Indian. There is, however, a marked difference in the two. The Egyptian depicts Mu falling into an abyss of fire, while the Nootka Indian depicts her as being submerged and covered with water. Two phases in her destruction and both correct.

The three divisions are deciphered as follows:

Top. The Serpent. This serpent has a plume of feathers on its head, it is therefore an adorned serpent, the well known Quetzalcoatl of the Mayas, and the symbol of the Deity as the Creator among the northern people of Mu. Thus the picture commences by saying that the Creator is dominating what is proceeding below.

Middle. The Thunder Bird. Thunder Bird legends permeate the tales of the Indians of the Northwest. Birds were one of the symbols, symbolizing the four great Primary Forces which are the executors of the Deity's commands. Birds were the favored symbol to express these Forces in the Northern parts of Mu, while to the south crosses were more frequently used. While Birds were not the favorite symbol in the more southern parts of Mu, yet, as I have said before, they were not excluded by any of the ancient peoples.

Bottom. The Killer Whale. This division is the crux of the whole picture—the top and middle amounts to but a preliminary setting.

The Killer Whale is purely a conventional fish, just a symbol. The eye is made out of the compound symbol mother and land which, conjoined, reads Motherland. The pupil is a solid black square symbolizing darkness, therefore the Motherland is in darkness.

The neck is shown as broken, with the symbol, abyss and magnetic Forces, falling from the wings of the Thunder Bird (the Four Great Forces) into the broken neck, thus showing that it is subsidiary forces coming from the Primary that is accomplishing the destruction.

Within the mouth is the symbol for flowing water, at the end of the mouth a passageway is shown, beyond this passage way is the hieratic letter U, the alphabetical symbol for an abyss, thus saying the Motherland has been carried down into an abyss of water. Directly following the abyss is the Uighur numeral four, four bars. On the backbone is the Naga form of number four, four circles or disks. The number four was the numeral symbol for the Four Great Primary Forces. Above the backbone are five bars, the Uighur way of writing five. Five was the numeral symbol of the full or monotheistic godhead.

Legend. Thus repeating within the fish what was said by top and middle figures. The whole as a legend would read: the Creator ordered or commanded the submergence of Mu. His executors the Four Primary Forces proceeded to carry out the command by dispatching subsidiary Forces to do the work. These caused the land to sink and the waters to cover over the sunken land.

CHAPTER VIII

THE MOUND BUILDERS OF NORTH AMERICA

NONE of the prehistoric races that have inhabited North America have caused more interest and speculation than the Mound Builders. Among their remains, in their mounds and burial grounds, have been found pottery of a high order, bone needles with eyes, stone pipes with elbows, strings of fine beads made from shells, fragments of cloth, ornaments of catlinite, silver, copper and tortoise shell, and some strings of extraordinarily large pearls, etc.[1]

On their ornaments and pottery are found various religious symbols, connecting them with a prehistoric race in Mexico and with Mu, the Motherland of Man. By these symbols it is shown that they possessed a highly scientific knowledge, for they perfectly understood the great Cosmic Sciences which today are just dawning on our scientific world. The Cosmic Sciences include the origin and workings of the Four Great Primary Forces, the parents of all forces. My object is not to attempt to give a history of the Mound Builders but simply to give some of the high lights about them which

[1] The pearls, fragments of cloth, ornaments of silver and copper were found in the Bainbridge Mound in Ohio.

apparently have been overlooked by the archaeological authorities who have been keeping the public informed regarding the mysteries of the Mound Builders. My object is to show their great civilization, which I think has been underestimated, and that they came from Mu via Mexico.

Regarding the time when they were living in America I have found nothing whereby even an approximate date could be suggested except that it was *after* Atlantis went down about 11,500 years ago. My opinion is that they were among the last of the prehistoric races that can be called prehistoric.

Geographically they occupied what may be termed the Mississippi Watershed. This area before the sinking of Atlantis was a shallow inland sea extending north from the Gulf of Mexico. The sinking of Atlantis in the Atlantic Ocean formed an immense hole in the Atlantic. To fill this in and level off the waters the surrounding waters were drawn in. This drew off the waters from various shallow inland seas, made them either dry habitable lands, or swamps. It also extended the coast lines. During the process of the readjustment of the waters the Mississippi Valley was drained. Even after the land was drained it was a long time before it assumed a condition where man could live and thrive upon it. This condition seems verified by the fact that no remains of the Cliff Dwellers, or those that preceded them, have been discovered in the Mississippi Valley proper.

The end of the Mound Builders, like the Khymers of Cambodia, apparently came very suddenly, leaving no trace behind it. While the Mound Builders show no cause for their apparent sudden disappearance the Khymers do, for it is geologically shown that the Khymers were destroyed by a flood, a cataclysmic wave having rolled up the Meikong River and surrounding Khymer country.

The Mound Builders as a people are gone, but did they leave no descendants in America? If Sacred Symbols, which I have found the most reliable source with which to trace the movements of people from time to time, are acceptable (I say this after fifty years of study), then we have something with which to make a start. This, with other evidence which may hereafter be found, may eventually show that they have descendants still among us in some of the Indian tribes of our southwestern states.

Fig. 1. Is a bottle recovered from a mound on a line between Southeast Missouri and Arkansas. Therefore, this is of ancient workmanship.

Fig. 2. Is a water bottle I personally own. It was bought from Indians in New Mexico within the last ten years and was perfectly new when given to me. This, therefore, is modern. The main figure on each of these two bottles is identical, with the exception of coloring. The ancient has a creamy white ground with brilliant figures. The modern has a brick red ground with black figures edged with white.

The symbol referred to is the same, line for line, and is an artistic design of the cross symbolizing the Sacred Four, the Four Great Primary Forces. The lines of the cross are drawn to extend in westerly directions, thus running from west to east. This is also shown on some of the Mexican tablets.

There is evidence that the Mound Builders of North

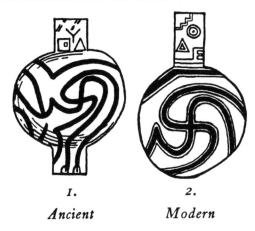

I.   *2.*

Ancient   *Modern*

America had an advanced knowledge of the Cosmic Forces which they could have attained only by some connection with, or direct, from the Motherland. Thus it is shown that their forefathers came from Mu, but by what gate did they enter America? I find among the traditions and lore of the Indians who now are on the lands where the mounds are found that: *"The Mound Builders came to the Mississippi Valley from Mexico."* Can these traditions of the Indians which say that the Mound Builders came to North America from Mexico be proven?

THE SACRED SYMBOLS OF MU

I already have shown one example where an ancient prehistoric people of Mexico had the same symbols as the Mound Builders, conveying identically the same meaning in both cases. By comparing other symbols of the Mound Builders with those found carved on Niven's Mexican tablets it appears to show some definite connection between them, and that these Indian legends are history, orally handed down.

Water Bottle
From a mound, Mississippi County, Missouri

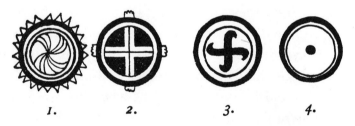

1.   *2.*   *3.*   *4.*

As an example, I will take the symbols found on another Mound Builder's water bottle and compare them with some of the symbols on the Mexican tablets. Here we find an exceedingly strong link connecting the American Mound Builders with the prehistoric race of Mexico, heretofore referred to.

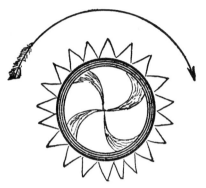

Symbol of the construction and workings of the Sun

This symbol is one of many found on a Mound Builder's water jar in Mississippi County, Missouri, and is a diagram showing how the Forces of the Sun are generated and carried throughout the Solar System. The dissection of it shows:

That the Sun has a hard crust and a soft center.

That the Sun is being revolved by her Superior Sun from west to east.

The revolving hard crust carries around the soft center in the same direction, but not at the same velocity, thus forming a frictional line, a magnet. This is shown by the soft material in the center being curved.

It is shown to refer to the Four Great Primary Forces by the central soft material being divided into four arms forming a cross, the first and original symbols of the Four Great Forces.

The form of the rays of the Sun are in the shape of the symbol for activity, thus saying that the rays are active in carrying the Forces somewhere, *i.e.,* the generated Forces are taken from the hard crust by the rays and delivered in a manner to carry out certain functions not shown in this diagram.

This diagram of the American Mound Builders is the only one I have come across so far that fully carries out the writings about this phase of the Sun, which are found in the Books of the Golden Age, and thus showing the excellence of the scientific knowledge of the Mound Builders of America. Many of the Mexican tablets give parts of it but none in whole as does this one. Writings from Egypt show that they understood the Cosmic Forces in 1200 B. C., but how much later I cannot say.

The Mound Builders of America date back to when? This brings forward a question—since when were the Cosmic Sciences lost to the world? Yet, they have never been entirely lost. The old Rishi understood them. Scraps of them still are known in the Orient and among the Polynesians, and I am not so sure that some scraps are not known among some of the tribes of the North American Indians. I have good reasons for saying this. In this diagram the Sun is drawn as representative of Kin, the Celestial Orb, and not as Ra, the monotheistic symbol of the Deity.

The foregoing are definitely the teachings found in the Sacred Writings.

This is a compound cross symbolizing the Sun as the Celestial Orb with a white cross in the center surmounted with a red cross. The white open cross reads *U luumil,* which translated is the Country of, the Land of, the Empire of—and being within the Sun, reads—the Empire of the Sun, Mu.

The plain cross surmounting the white open cross is the oldest and original symbol for the Four Great Primary Forces, sometimes depicted with the Swastika, subsequently termed the "Good Luck" symbol.

Mound Builders   *Mexican*

*Showing the Four Primary Forces moving
from West to East*

I have selected just one of the Mexican Tablets to show beside a Mound Builder's symbol, Niven's No. 1231. I have taken this Mexican tablet for comparison as I have hitherto, in various of my writings, stated that this tablet was one of the most important among

Niven's collection of over 3000, and one of the most important finds in any part of the world.

In both cases the Mound Builders and the Mexican show the Four Great Primary Forces emanating from the Creator, and are said by the ancients "To be His commands, His desires, His wishes." They are, in both symbols, shown moving from west to east, thus causing the whole universe to revolve from west to east, and all living moving spheres to revolve on their axes from west to east.

This is a universal symbol found in all ancient countries throughout the world. It is a picture of the Sun as Ra, the monotheistic symbol of the Deity.

MOUND BUILDERS' SYMBOLS.—

Line 1. Figs. 1 to 5. All these symbols are pictures of the Sun, and are universal, that is, they are found among the writings of all ancient peoples.

Line 2. Figs. 6 to 10. These five symbols are all recording the Four Great Primary Forces, and that they emanate from the Creator. Figs. 6, 7, and 8 are frequently found among Niven's Mexican tablets, and in the Mexican they are always shown as originating from the demand or order of the Creator. Figs. 9 and 10 are more universally found among ancient writings.

Line 3. Figs. 11 to 15. These figures symbolize the

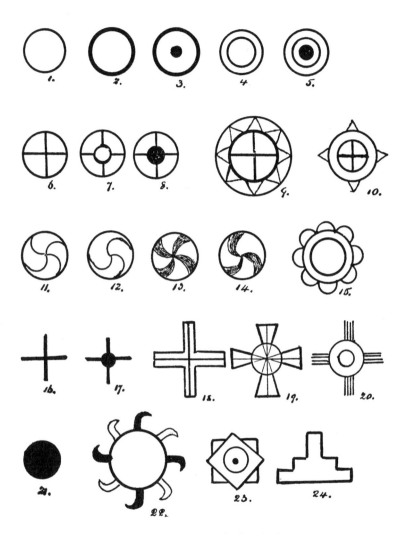

Mound Builders' Symbols

earth's Forces and their origin and the manner in which they work. Figs. 11 and 12 are skeleton, or outline, drawings of 13 and 14. These four figures show the earth's molten center being carried around and grinding against the earth's hard crust. This grinding forms a frictional line between the two, which in turn forms a magnet. The magnet has two divisions, one affecting Forces, the other, elementary matter. The Division, having control over elements, is what is commonly known as the Force of Gravity, therefore, what is known as the Force of Gravity is the power of the Cold Division of the Earth's great Central Dual Magnet. The Division, having power over Forces, affects the *Earth's Forces only*. It has no control over any Forces emanating from beyond the earth's atmosphere. Fig. 15 shows the earth's Forces passing out of her body into the atmosphere (they are thus drawn out by their affinitive Forces carried in the Sun's rays). Earthly Forces like elements become exhausted, and when exhausted the Sun's affinitive Forces have no further attraction or control over them. The Central Magnet then proceeds to draw them back into the great frictional line where they are regenerated and again sent to perform the duties required of them by nature. I may say further that this example of the workings and origin of earthly Forces may also apply to all revolving bodies throughout the universe, and thus show that a single Divine system is controlling the Universe.

Line 4. Figs. 16 to 20. These are also symbols of

the Four Great Primary Forces. Figs. 17, 19 and 20 are shown as emanating from the Deity. Fig. 16 is the original and oldest symbol for the Sacred Four or the Four Great Primary Forces as it is found in the Sacred Writings of Mu, which are more than 70,000 years old. All of these symbols are found embodied in the Mexican tablets. Fig. 19 is an exact duplicate of what I have heretofore given as the Pyramid Cross.

Line 5. Figs. 21 to 24. In this line I shall note only one figure, 22. The others are common and universal. Fig. 22 is a very rare symbol. I have found only one duplicate of it, and that is the Hindu writings of about 4000 to 5000 years ago. This figure symbolizes the Sun sending forth his rays throughout his System (the solar). They are shown as being of two varieties—dark and invisible because of their intensity, and light, which are apparent to vision. The rays are in the form of Forces, as shown by the Force symbol. Again they are curved, pointing to the east and thereby telling us that they are working from west to east and forming a circle. As they are taking a circular route all rays coming from the Sun would not strike the earth in a straight line from the Sun but in a curve.

This again shows that our prehistoric Americans were further advanced in science than we are today. Do our present scientists appreciate this fact? Does this not show that we are thousands of years behind in our knowledge of science, based on theory alone? Personally, I think so.

*A Mound Builder's Calendar Stone
Found in the Ouachita River,
Hot Springs, Arkansas*

From Col. J. R. Fordyce, Little Rock, Arkansas

A MOUND BUILDER'S CALENDAR STONE.—

Dimensions. The stone is pear shaped. Length about 16 inches, and about 13 inches across at its widest part. "It is a sandstone bowlder such as found in shale near Hot Springs. It weighs 22½ pounds."

Description. In the center is a slightly raised ring 7¼ inches in diameter. This ring is divided into thirteen equal divisions. On each division is inscribed a figure or a glyph. Superimposed on this circle is another which is much higher. This, I presume to be meant for a picture of the Sun, as the symbol of the Deity. Above this main figure is engraved a caption, the Moon in its various phases during a calendar month. This tells us the meaning of what is below, namely: the circle with the thirteen divisions represents thirteen calendar months, making one year. The thirteen

230

months, forming a circle, tell us that the year is completed, the beginning and the end. Over the caption is shown the All Seeing Eye looking down from heaven above. This is an ancient symbol dating back to the earliest writings, and universally found. Outside of the calendar proper, to the edge of the stone, various animals are shown, including Man.

The Calendar Glyphs.

1. This is too indistinct to say positively what is meant or represented. However, it appears to be a bird with wings outspread. If this is correct, then it probably would be the American Indian Thunder Bird.

2. This seems to portray the Maya month of Zac, the white month, when snow covers the ground with a white blanket.

3. This is a new symbol to me. I do not know its meaning.

4. This is a fish which is symbolically heading upstream, denoting that during this month fish are most plentiful, the time when they make their spring run up to their spawning beds.

5. This glyph is one of the letters in Mu's alphabet. It has an esoteric meaning.

6. This is a picture of the Sacred Lotus flower, Mu's floral symbol. The lotus was the most beloved and revered of all Mu's symbols. The Egyptians always referred to Mu as the Lotus.

7. Without this is a line drawing of the head of the Mound Builders' conventional serpent. I do not know what it is. Among the etchings at the Pipestone Quarry, Minnesota, there are some that are almost identically like it. The Pipestone are without question the heads of the Serpent.

8. This is a sacred symbol common in Oriental countries. Once, and only once, before have I found it in America. That was among the Mound Builders' remains taken from one of their burial grounds. It is one of those ancient religious symbols whose meaning was lost when the Brahmins persecuted and drove their teachers, the Naacals, out of India into the snow-capped ranges of the Himalayas about 2000 to 2500 B. C. The meaning of the symbol is expressed in four words of the ancient tongue. These words were used before the commencement of a supplication, or prayers. They are being repeated to this day but the priesthood does not know their meaning. The meaning of AUM was forgotten about the same date. So far in months 6 and 8 we find a direct connection between the people who made this calendar stone and the *Mound Builders, Mu* and the *Orient.*

9. This glyph is new to me. It appears to picture ripe grain being cut and harvested. The time on this stone is given about August or September. It would thus correspond with harvest time when grain is reaped and stored.

10. This symbol is frequently found in ancient writings. It pictures the fall of the year when trees and shrubs shed their leaves, leaving the branches bare and leafless.

11. This is one of the most conclusive symbols on this stone and directly connects the makers of this stone calendar with the *Mound Builders,* the *Polynesians,* and therefore, *Mu,* as their ancestors came from the Motherland. The symbol is the Grey and Black Pointed Spider, which is discussed later in this chapter. I have received information that similar spiders have been found among the treasures recovered by Schliemann in ancient Troy, Asia Minor. These, however, I have not seen.

12. This symbol is questionable. Is it the outline of a deer?

13. This is certainly an outline drawing of a bison. It is now the last month in the year, the head of this buffalo is pointing in. Is this the time of the year when food has become scarce further north and he is now working in to the south where conditions for the time being suit him better? I think so. The same question applies to the 12th, the deer.

Comments. There are various animals shown on the outer side of the stone. These I have not taken into account although two are very prominent in ancient picture writings and in Indian legends.

It must be apparent that the designers of this Calendar Stone were acquainted with the Cosmic Forces and the Cosmic Sciences as taught during the First

Great Civilization. Therefore, America at one time was enjoying the highest civilization the earth has ever known.

THE GREAT SERPENT MOUNDS.—The feature which has captivated the public interest most in the Mound Builders is their great serpent-shaped mounds. That these serpent mounds were symbolical there can be no doubt. Serpents of various patterns and designs have always, from the beginning of religion, played an important part in religious ceremonies, not among one particular race but among *all* ancient people from the time symbols were first used.

One of the most important of the American Serpent Mounds is situated at Brush Creek near Peebles, Ohio. I cannot say definitely in what way this Serpent Mound was symbolically used—whether as the Seven Great Commands of Creation, the Waters, or the destruction of Mu, the Motherland. Possibly it may have included two of the foregoing. That it, or ceremonies connected with it, referred to Mu there is ground for belief for the following reason: it is stated that some of the Serpent Mounds have sacrificial stones or altars upon them, with the possibility that all had them originally. As Mu went down it was into "a fiery abyss," fires of the underneath. It became a custom among all surviving peoples thereafter at various times and occasions to commemorate her destruction by fire. Fire is shown to have been used in commemorative services by the Mayas and Quiches who had their fiery house, and the

Egyptians who used a fiery tank, and others who used burnt sacrifices of some description.

In England near Stonehenge there is a Serpent Mound said to be an exact duplication of the American at Peebles, Ohio. Thus, we find in England a specialized symbol of the same as used by the Mound Builders of America, and in both cases the same meaning and conception is conveyed. What is a reasonable deduction? Common origin, without doubt. By what route did the Mound Builders get into England? It is questionable when we trace the various symbols that have been found in England, and the still more pronounced display found in Egypt.

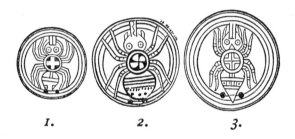

I.   2.   3.

SPIDERS.—While the great Serpent Mounds have captured the most public interest among the Mound Builders' relics, the Spiders have the greatest fascination for me, personally. While exploring among the South Sea Islands some fifty years ago I constantly came across legends about the Grey and Black Pointed Spider. These legends showed that the Spider was symbolic of something, and that it was a sacred symbol,

but of what I could not determine. The legends were all
too obtuse. As examples:

"There the Grey and Black Pointed Spider would
have mounted to Heaven, but he was held back by the
bitterness of the cold."

"The roads were cunningly constructed to represent
the web of the Grey and Black Pointed Spider, and no
man could discover the beginning or the end thereof."

Now after waiting fifty years and having given up all
hope of ever solving the riddle of the Grey and Black
Pointed Spider I find the answer given at our very
doorstep. Truly, here in America lies the key to un-
lock the great past history of man.

These Spiders were brought to my notice by my
friend, Dr. Thomas M. Stewart, of Cincinnati, Ohio.
They are engraved on circular pieces of shell, and on
each of their backs is a symbol showing what they
represented. These peculiar relics have been found in
the burial vaults of the Mound Builders of Missouri,
Arkansas and Tennessee. Because of the location of
the places where they have been found Dr. Stewart
suggested that they might have been used in the same
manner as the Scarab in the Egyptian burial chambers.

The symbols on the backs of these Spiders are du-
plications of the symbols found as ornaments on the
Water Bottle shown on page 241. No. 1 is the original
symbol for the Four Great Forces shown in No. 2 on
page 241. No. 2 shows the Forces working from west

to east as in No. 3 on page 241. No. 3 is the same compound symbol as shown in No. 2, page 241.

Some of these symbols are shown on pottery recovered from the ancient ruined cities in Crete, Cyprus and ancient Troy [1] in Asia Minor.

Although exceedingly rare, I think that the Grey and Black Spider, as a symbol, had a wide range at one time and we still may find many of them on pottery that have been overlooked because their import was unknown.

I think that the foregoing bears out my assertion that merely digging up old remains, symbols, inscriptions and writings is not archaeology, that archaeology is the reading of these symbols and writings when found. A builder, digging a foundation for a structure, who unearths a stone bearing an ancient inscription does not make the builder an archaeologist—he is only a builder. A farmer, ploughing his ground, turns over an old stone with an inscription on it. This does not make the farmer an archaeologist—he is only a cultivator of the soil. Or his son may be digging potatoes and unearth an old piece of pottery. The son is only a potato digger, not an archaeologist.

The Mound Builders' Symbols, before they are read, are only artistic ornamentations and mean nothing, just potatoes on a piece of pottery. But, when read, they may give a line on a page of the early history of North

[1] Schliemann's "Treasures of Priam."

America by telling us that a mysterious race called the Mound Builders, who once occupied a part of our land, originally came from Mu via Mexico, that they were a highly civilized and enlightened people, having a knowledge of the Cosmic Forces and their workings, thus showing that they had a scientific knowledge greater than we have today.

The Octopus, a Sacred Symbol

THE OCTOPUS.—The Octopus is one of the very rare sacred symbols. By this I do not mean that it was seldom used, but that only a few symbols of it have been found. As a matter of fact I think it was a very common symbol among some of the ancient peoples. At present when found, generally on pottery, archaeologists have looked upon them as mere decorations and ignored the fact that many of the specimens show, without a doubt, that they were sacred symbols (Plate VI).

The Octopus is often found on the ancient Greek pottery. It was used in Peru, Brazil, North America, Greece and Scandinavia until a few thousand years ago. Judging by the way it was used it was the symbol of a *Water Demon, the Enemy of Life*. Its rôle was to prevent the advent of life on earth.

Most of the ancient writings telling about the advent of life on earth symbolize it in such a manner that it represents a battle between the Sun and the Waters for supremacy over something, but does not say what that something is.

For example: the Babylonians say Belmarduk, the Sun, fights Tiamet, the Waters. From a Cuneiform Tablet—"The gods are preparing for a grand contest against the monster, Tiamet." "The god Belmarduk overthrows Tiamet." The Egyptians have it that Horus, the Sun, overcomes and kills the serpent Aphopis, the Waters. The Hindus say that Krisna, the Sun, destroyed the serpent Anatha, the Waters. And the Greeks record that Apollo, the Sun, overcomes Python, the Waters. The Fifth Command of the Sacred Writings of Mu is: "And the arrows of the Sun met the arrows of the Earth in *the mud of the waters* and out of particles of the mud formed cosmic eggs"—life germs.

From the foregoing, combined with the legends about the Octopus, it appears that the Octopus was the symbol of the *resistance* of the mud against allowing the Sun's Forces to draw the Earth's Forces out into the water to form life's cosmic eggs. The Sun's Forces, however, prevailed and met the Earth's Forces and formed cosmic eggs, and life commenced according to Divine Command.

The legends as told today about the Octopus are perfect myths, but by going behind the myth and finding its origin we discover the true legend.

It was very noticeable that wherever a legend is found the phenomenon is shown to have occurred in that particular spot. This is especially so among savage and semi-savage people. As examples: the Fijians have

239

a legend about the "Tower of Babel." According to them the "Tower of Babel" was being built on one of the Fijian Islands. The Fijians are courteous to visitors and will take anyone gladly to the spot where it stood. The Polynesians have a legend about the "Ark." They claim that it was built on one of their islands. The Maoris have a legend about "Cain and Abel." They tell you that Cain and Abel were New Zealanders and that the murder of Abel occurred in New Zealand.

The symbolic Octopus, like the Sun, is known by many names, its name being taken from the language of the people where it is found. With all people the Octopus was a *Water Demon* and *the Enemy of Life.* It had no other meaning.

SHADOWS FROM GREECE AND ASIA MINOR.—From the ancient cities of the Grecian Archipelago and Asia Minor, which have been and are being unearthed, many pieces of pottery have been found which have the Octopus either engraved, raised or painted on them, making prominent and striking decorations. In Crete, Cyprus and Troy many fine and perfect specimens have been discovered. Fortunately, the motif designs vary considerably which gives one a fair chance to read their correct meaning, as for instance, on vases B and C in the Cyprus Group. On both the tentacles and body are intact. Here the Octopus is simply a reminder of that which it symbolizes. Vase A, from the same ruined city, shows a totally different phase. Here the Octopus is depicted as having been in battle and got the worst of the encounter. This is shown by his broken and cut tentacles, his fighting weapons.

A.

B.   *C.*

A group of octopus vases from Cyprus

From where did the Greeks get the Octopus? First, the Octopus appears to have been one of the symbols used by Mu. From the Motherland it was taken by the Carians into Peru and Brazil. Second, when the Carians, the forefathers of the Greeks, continued their advance towards the east and finally settled at the eastern end of the Mediterranean they carried their sacred symbols along with them and among these was the Octopus.

I think the foregoing shows sufficient proof that the Octopus was one of the early sacred symbols and that it was carried to the southeastern parts of Europe and Asia Minor by the Carians. But what people carried it to Scandinavia is an open question.

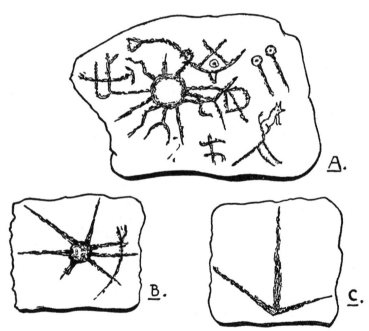

The Pipestone Octopus
Witoonti, Pipestone, Minnesota

THE PIPESTONE OCTOPUS.—In trying to read this pictograph one apparently is met by three contradictions: First, the Octopus has within the grasp of one of its upper tentacles a Serpent, a specialized Serpent, an exact duplication of one of the Mound Builders' Serpent Mounds. What connection is there between the Mound Builders and the people who carved this rock picture? Were they the same people? Or was this peculiar specialized Serpent used by various peoples and was this picture etched by one of them? The Octopus, having the Serpent within the grasp of one of its tentacles, intimates that the circle from which the tentacles project is the body of the Octopus; but being a circle it is a picture of the Sun. This would suggest that the circle was a Sun symbol and not the body of the Octopus.

Second, as against reading the circle as a Sun symbol we see projecting from the lower side of the circle the beak of the Octopus in the form of the ancient symbol for a cutting or dividing Force. This symbol also appears on the Mexican tablet No. 1584, Woman's Creation. Added to this in the small Fig. B, the Octopus is shown with a real body, nearly round, with the Serpent held in one of the tentacles.

Third, the foregoing shows a possibility that the circle forming the body in Fig. A may actually be symbolizing the Sun's Forces as Kin, the Celestial orb, and not Ra, the monotheistic symbol of the Deity.

One of the difficulties in attempting to read this picture is that the ends of most of the tentacles are so indistinct that their meanings are doubtful. This picture requires a great deal of study with the assistance of other pictures referring to the same subject to obtain the full meaning in detail. The fact remains that it may convey the same meaning as the Octopus on the Cyprus Vase A and many other pictures of the Greeks, Egyptians, Hindus, Babylonians, etc.

At the lower right hand corner is shown either a wolf or a dog. In the Scandinavian myths this dog or wolf plays an important part.

THE PIPESTONE QUARRY.—This quarry in Pipestone, Minnesota, is the oldest quarry on earth to have been worked by man, for it was known and worked back in the Tertiary Era, before the mythical Glacial Period, the last Magnetic Cataclysm.

Gilders Pipe, Omaha, Nebraska, over 15,000 years old, made out of the red mottled stone of Pipestone Quarry

The age of the Pipestone Quarry is proven by two facts. First, by Gilders Pipe which was found among the remains of man who lived during the Tertiary Era. The clay from which this pipe is made is found only at one spot on earth (as far as is known to geology), and that is at Pipestone. The geological name of this

244

stone is Catlinite. (It has been claimed by some that Catlinite is also found at Feuerte Farm about three miles from Portsmouth, Ohio. The only way that this can be decided satisfactorily is by comparing the chemical analysis of the two—the Pipestone deposit and that found at Portsmouth.)

According to Indian traditions the location of the Pipestone Quarry was lost for a long period of time. Its rediscovery forms one of the Sioux legends. The Indian legends about the Pipestone and other subjects are fascinating, and when shorn of their mythical adornments tell us that the first Americans came from Mu, which adds another link to the overwhelming chain of evidence that America was Mu's first colony and that America today is the oldest land above water that has been inhabited by man. America antedates Atlantis, Egypt, Greece, Babylonia, India and all other ancient nations. The Pipestone Indian legends also show that the first Americans were highly civilized people, and that they came from a land in the west beyond the Setting Sun.

In reference to the rediscovery of the quarry, Omaha and Yaukton Indian legends relate that "Walregela, the Omaha wife of a Yaukton Sioux, following the trail of a white bison discovered the Pipestone on the banks of the Pipestone Creek, where it had been exposed by the bison's hoofs."

Extracts from Chon-oopa-sa.—Legend by Pa-la-ne-a-pa-pe (Man that was struck by the Ra).

THE SACRED SYMBOLS OF MU

The Advent of Man

"In the far off past
A million, million, million moons ago,
The first of mortals to this earth below
    By great Wo-kon was cast:
The first Dakota moulded from a star
    He tossed and watched him fall
Down through the dark, till he alighted there
    Upon soft ground. He was not hurt at all
    And Wa-kin-yan, first Sioux."

"He ranged the land in hunting many a year
Until at last this solitary man"

*"Where afar we see the sunset
Summer days* in golden glory
In *the mystic land of legend*
In that far land of *the west*
Land of Red-man's home and story.
Land of legend, strange *tradition,*
Vale of dim *unwritten hist'ry."*

The Woman

"And Wa-kin-yan prayed hourly (never tired . . .)
Wa-kon to send him what he most desired . . .
And Wa-kon heard his pleading,—broke a beam

THE MOUND BUILDERS

At noon from off the blazing summer Sun
And moulded, fashioned—beauteous as a dream,—
The first of all her sex—the longed for One!
. . . Sweet Co-tan-ka—"

The Demon Octopus

"Wi-toon-ti, he that stayed
By day in the river's *mud.*"

"Wi-toon-ti, he that feared
Wa-kin-yan's bow and shaft."

"A monster he."

"Then Wa-kon-da, vengeance taking
For the murdered Sunbeam's daughter."

"Then he seized a blazing tail star
Formed another mighty arrow
Sent it flying to Wa-kin-yan."

"The Wa-kin-yan rose up quickly
By the blazing shaft he sighted!
Twang! behold it forward flying
See it flare and flash and hurtle
Through the rain of fiery sparks
Through Wi-toon-ta . . ."

This appears to me to be another version of the fight between the Sun and the Waters, for the creation of Life, so frequently found in the ancient writings on the Creation.

While other Indian legends refer to Mu none of them say what she and her people were like or where she lay except that she was "Beyond the Setting Sun." This Sioux legend goes further—it describes the land as being tropical "Summer days in golden glory." That the teller of the legend was cognizant of the fact that Mu had disappeared and was no more is shown in the passage, "The mystic land of legend." It also tells us that legends about her greatness and civilization were being orally handed down. "Land of Red-man's home and story" informs us that the Indians know that originally they came from Mu. "Dim unwritten hist'ry" tells us that as far as the Indian knows there is no written history of Mu, only legendary.

Another interesting bit of Pipestone lore is the symbolic Bird of Creation. Here at Pipestone among the Sioux legends we again find the Bird of Creation the symbol of the Creative Forces throughout the world. Catlin, in 1836, recounting his visit to the Pipestone, says: "Not far from us, in the solid rock, are the deeply impressed footprints of the Great Spirit in the form of the tracks of a Great Bird. (See Fig. C. Page 242.)

The following are extracts from a Sioux legend: *"Before* the creation of man, the Great Spirit, whose tracks are yet to be seen on the stones of the Red Pipe in the form of that of a great bird."

"Here the Great Spirit used to slay the buffaloes and eat them on the edge of the rock. The blood running over the rocks turned them red."

"One day a large *snake* had crawled into the nest of the bird to eat his eggs. One of the eggs hatched out in a clap of thunder, and the Great Spirit catching hold of a piece of pipestone to throw at the snake (here part of the legend missing) moulded it into a man. The man's feet grew fast in the ground, where *it* stood fast for many ages like a great *tree,* therefore he grew very old. (In all of the ancient pictures of Mu she is depicted as a very old woman.) At last another *tree* grew up beside him when a large *snake* ate them both off at the *roots* and they wandered off together. From these have sprung all the people now on earth." Here we have two of the ancient writings merged into one—the Advent of Man on Earth, and the Destruction of Mu.

Although no particular name has been given to the Great Bird in this Sioux legend beyond the Great Spirit I think that by its connection with thunder it was the Thunder Bird of all the Indians to the west of the Sioux and was, as told by the old Hayden chief, the symbol of the Creative Forces. The Great Bird eating buffaloes is without question a perfect myth invented by some old Medicine Man to save his face when pressed by his followers to account for the pipestone being red. The legend says *before* man came on earth the Great Spirit used to slay buffalos to eat. First, spirits do not eat anything material. Second, it occurred before man was on earth, "A million, million, million moons ago." And third, the buffalo is a recent addition to the picture gallery of life of America.

Man first appeared on Mu. One of the names given to Mu was the *Tree* of Life. In this legend the man and the tree are combined in one. Yet this is not so far wrong, for the Sacred Writings of Mu tell us that Mu was the Tree of Life and that Man was its fruit. This is corroborated where the Sioux legend tells of a great *serpent* biting off the trees at their roots. A serpent was always the symbol for the waters and when Mu was destroyed she was swallowed by the waters. Biting, in the Sioux legend, is a correct word to use symbolically, for Mu was certainly bitten off from the rest of the land above water. "From these have sprung all the people that now inhabit the earth" clearly shows that this refers to the migrated children of Mu and is confirmed by the saying, "They wandered off" for they had left the land of their birth where they grew up, to go to other lands where they might find living easier.

All extracts, pictures and information about the Pipestone are taken from a booklet entitled, *The Pipestone Indian Shrine,* by Miss Winifred Bartlett, President of the Pipestone Indian Shrine Association, who kindly and courteously sent me the booklet from which to make notes, with a view of placing America where it belongs on the ancient map, and to give the Redskin his just due. The translations of the Indian legends are by D. Ivan Downs.

CHAPTER IX

RELIGION IN EGYPT AND INDIA

THE EGYPTIAN PANTHEON.—Many of our religious conceptions today are strong reflections of the old Egyptian. One might say indeed that our present day religion came to us from Egypt via the Jews. For that reason I have decided to give in this book an Egyptian Pantheon, which I have made up from the Egyptian Book of the Dead.

In many cases, it will be seen that the symbol of a certain belief or conception is represented by more than one god shown in the Pantheon. Under different guises and different names they, however, symbolize but a single conception. This comes from the scrambling of two sets of symbols when Upper and Lower Egypt were joined and became one kingdom.

I am giving 24 figures placing them 6 on a page for easy reference. There are many others which I have not included; these are the principal ones only. I can only give an outline description, space will not permit of more. If more data is required about them, it will be found in many books written about Egypt.

Amen was the great god at Thebes, and was ad-

dressed as the "King of the gods." The Latinized form of the name is Ammon. The Romans identified him with Jupiter. The Greeks called him Zeus. He is also called "the hidden god." Before the 18th Dynasty he was worshipped at Thebes as *Amen* simply; but was afterwards merged into *Amen Ra:* "the hidden Sun." His color was a light blue.

Kneph was called "the moulder." He was known by the Greeks as Knonphis. Kneph is one of the oldest of the Egyptian gods and was especially worshipped in Nubia and Philae. His headdress is a ram's head surmounted with a solar disk and uraeus. Kneph is spoken of as "the soul of the Universe" and "The Creator." His color was bright green. Kneph's female consort was Sati.

Sati was the female consort of Kneph, and was looked upon as the Egyptian Juno. Her principal seat of worship was Elephantine, and throughout Nubia and Ethiopia. Her headdress was the Crown of Upper Egypt with a pair of cow's horns extending from it. Sati's color was a warm red human flesh color. I think that there can be no question but what Kneph and Sati were intended to symbolize the two principles of the Creator: male and female.

Khem was one of the deified attributes of the Creator. His special seat of worship was Chemmo (Panopolis). He was worshipped at Thebes and to some extent throughout Egypt. His headdress consisted of two straight feathers. He was generally colored blue.

"Ptah the Opener" was the oldest of the Egyptian gods. His principal seat of worship was at Memphis. Ptah was the symbol of the Creative power of the Deity. The Egyptians called him "the divine artificer."

One of his symbols was the two-sided square. ⌐

He had many titles; one was: "The Father of beginnings." The Greeks considered Ptah the same as their Vulcan. His name, peculiar to Memphis, was Ptah-Sokar-Osiris. The regular Egyptian name, however, was Ptah-Sekar-Usar. His color was blue. Ptah was without doubt the symbol of the Four Great Primary Forces— The Sacred Four.

Neith was the Egyptian Minerva, and was the goddess of the lower heavens. She is generally pictured holding up the heavens on her head. Neith was the special goddess at Sais. A corresponding symbol—a god upholding the heavens on his head—is found in the Maya of Yucatan. His color was blue. Neith was the symbol of The Four Great Pillars that upheld the Universe—The Sacred Four.

Maut called "the Mother" was the consort of Amen Ra at Thebes, and in this capacity represented the Mother of all: thus in Amen Ra and Maut we find another symbolization of the dual principle of the Creator. Maut was especially worshipped at Thebes in connection with Amen and at Chons with Amen Ra. She was also honored throughout Nubia and Ethiopia. Her color was warm, flesh colored red.

255

MAUT.   RA.   KHEPRA.

ATUM.   SHU.   MENTU.

Ra was the name of the Sun as the monotheistic symbol of The Creator—monotheistic or collective. In the "Litany of Ra" he is called "the Supreme Power," "the *only* one," et cetera. To the initiated, he symbolized the power of the Deity; but to the populace he was stated to be a created god, the Son of Ptah and Neith. More errors have been made about this symbol by historians than any other symbol used by the ancients. His color was red.

Khepra. Although this symbol is found in the Egyptian Pantheon, it did not originate in Egypt but in the Motherland and was brought to Upper Egypt by the Nagas from the Motherland via Burma and India. The symbol is the Scarab beetle, which is placed over the head of a human figure in the Egyptian symbol. The Scarab symbolizes creative energy.

From the Papyrus Ani., King's Companion to Seti II: "Among the Egyptians, the Scarabeaus Beetle is no god, but one of the emblems of the Creator, because it rolls a ball of mud between its feet and sets therein its eggs to hatch. As the Creator rolls the world around, and causes it to produce life."

The foregoing passage is one that should be especially studied by students of the ancient past: for it shows us that the Egyptians up to the time of Seti 2nd understood the ancients' sciences and the workings of the Great Cosmic Forces, both of which are unknown to the scientists of today.

Before our sciences can advance to any perceptible

degree the present grotesque myths, the orthodox scientific teachings, must be abandoned and a study of the Four Great Primeval Forces made. On them the true sciences must be built up—sciences which teach us what life is and how it originates, the workings of the Four Great Forces throughout the Universe, with their origin, et cetera.

The vignette shows an engraving which I found in a very ancient Maya carving in India. It is thousands of years older than the first occupation of Egypt by man. The engraving is symbolical, as it shows the Creator symbolized by a Scarab, which is placed within rays of glory and rests on the symbol of Mu. Kneeling in adoration on either side of the rays is first man shown by his symbol Kèė the deer.

This vignette is taken from the Egyptian sacred book, the Book of the Dead. It symbolizes man in adoration of the Scarab Beetle as the symbol of the Creator. The Egyptian god Khepra undoubtedly comes out of the Nagas—Kèė.

Atum or Tum was the god of the setting Sun: otherwise Amenti—the Sun below the horizon.

Shu was the firstborn of Ra and Hathor and brother of Tefnut. Shu was looked upon as a symbol of the Celestial Forces. His color was generally black.

OSIRIS.   HATHOR.   ISIS.

SEB.   HORUS.   KHONS.

THOTH.   NEPHTHYS.   ANUBIS.

Mentu was one of the deified attributes of the Sun and often bears the name Mentu-Ra. He was merely a phase of Ra who with Atum symbolized the rising and the setting Sun. Mentu was the special protector of Egypt.

Osiris was one of the oldest of the Egyptian gods. Later in this chapter I shall give the history of Osiris and show who he was. In the text of the Book of the Dead it is stated that he was the son of Seb and Nut.

Hathor was simply another name for Isis and is represented with the attributes of Isis. She was sometimes called Isis Hathor. Hathor personified Nature with all that was true and beautiful in it—the female principle of the Creator.

Isis is the goddess of the triad—Osiris, Isis and Horus. In the triad she was the wife of Osiris.

Horus was the son of Osiris and Isis and symbolized the Sun.

Seb was the father of Osiris and Isis and was called "the father of gods." Tefnut was his consort. In Seb and Tefnut again we find the dual principles of the Creator symbolized.

Khons was worshipped at Thebes, and, with Amen and Maut, formed the Theban triad. Khons symbolized the moon; he wears the disk and crescent moon.

Thoth was the god of writing, learning, and medicine. It was he who composed the early and most important portions of the Book of the Dead. Thoth is *supposed* to be the Egyptian Hermes.

TEFNUT.   MA.   NU.

BAST.   SET.   ANUKA.

Nephthys was the sister of Isis and Osiris and consort of Set.

Anubis was the god of embalming and embalmed his father Osiris.

Tefnut was the goddess of the rain and dew. She held a conspicuous place among the contemporary deities of Thebes.

Ma or Maat was the goddess of truth. She represents the truth and justice of the Supreme God.

Nu or Nut. Nut is the feminine form of Nu. Nu was the father, Nut the mother—the life givers.

Bast was the wife of Ptah and with their son Tum or Atum formed the great triad of Memphis.

Set was the son of Nut and brother of Osiris. According to the myth he murdered Osiris.

Anuka was the third member of the triad of Thebaid, composed of Khnum (Kneph), Sati and Anuka.

OSIRIS.—Osiris was one of the oldest of the Egyptian gods. His worship was universal throughout Egypt at all times. Osiris was the representative of all that was good.

The myths in Egypt about Osiris are bewildering. They claim that Osiris was once the monarch of Upper and Lower Egypt. It is claimed that Osiris was buried at Philae—other towns claim his remains. According to all these myths, Osiris must have lived since the union of Upper and Lower Egypt was accomplished under Menes about 5,000 B. C.

Against this we find that Thoth, the founder of the

Osiris

Lower Egyptians taught at Sais the Osirian Religion
and this was 14,000 B. C. There were no kings of Egypt
for an immensely long period after Thoth's time.
Egypt was a sub-colony of the Motherland under direct control of the colonial empire—Atlantis.

Now let us see who Osiris actually was and the time
when he lived. In two Himalayan monasteries—one in
India, the other in Tibet—there are two Naacal tablets
belonging to the Sacred Inspired Writings of the
Motherland: they are identically the same, word for
word, were copied from the originals in the Motherland and brought to the continent of Asia by Naacal
missionaries. They belong to the historical section of
the Sacred Books. They relate:

"Osiris, when entering manhood, left the home of his
birth, Atlantis, and came to the motherland where he
entered one of the Naacal colleges. Here he studied the
religion and Cosmic Sciences of the Motherland. When
he passed his degree of Master and adept, he returned
to his own country, Atlantis. There he devoted his life
to the teachings of the people, the first religion of man,
and to weeding out and eliminating extravagances, inventions and misconceptions that had crept into the
religion of Atlantis under a rank priesthood."

Osiris became the Hieratic Head of Religion in
Atlantis which office he held during a long life. The
people loved and worshipped him for his gentleness,
goodness and kindness. They wished to dethrone Ou-
ranos the King and place Osiris on the throne. This

Osiris would not allow to be spoken of and so condemned the idea that it was abandoned.

He was murdered by a brother on account of jealousy—this was about 20,000 B. C. His name was so revered, and he so beloved, that at his death he was deified, and as a lasting monument to his name religion was called after him, viz., "The Osirian religion," just as today we have the Christian religion. I could not find the name of the brother who murdered him, so the probability is the Egyptians invented the name. Nor do I find anything about Isis and Nephthys, but it is mentioned that he had a son, who became the Hieratic Head of Atlantis at the death of his father. I do not, however, find his name.

Osiris and Christ taught identically the same religion. Some of their preachings are word for word, line for line, and sentence for sentence the same. Both learned from the same book—the Sacred Inspired Writings of the Motherland.

THE RELIGION OF EGYPT.—The first we know about the religion of Egypt is where an ancient record states that about 16,000 years ago Thoth, the son of an Atlantian Priest, planted the Egyptian colony at the mouth of the Nile, and at Sais on the banks of the Nile built a temple and taught the Osirian religion.

The Osirian religion as I have previously shown was the religion of Mu after Osiris had cleansed it of all the extravagances that had crept into it in Atlantis, 22,000 years ago, the religion being then called after

him the Osirian religion. When he died his son became
the hieratical head and was supposed to be called
Horus, but whether Horus was his actual name or a
title I cannot say, but a Horus was always the hieratical
head of the Osirian religion down to the time of Menes
or about 5,000 B. C. Thus it is shown that the religion
of Egypt commenced with that of the Motherland as
taught in the Sacred Inspired Writings.

From the time of Thoth down to the time of Menes,
the Egyptian colony was ruled by the church, under
the head of a Horus. The last Horus is recorded when
Menes took the throne.

Manetho, the Egyptian priest historian, says that
during the 11th Dynasty the priesthood began to teach
the people to worship the Sacred Symbols instead of
the Diety Himself as heretofore. This was the first step
to the debauchery of the Egyptian religion which
reached its peak during the 18th Dynasty and ended in
every conceivable extravagance coupled with idolatry.
The advent of Mohammedanism wiped out the old religion of Egypt, although the Christian religion had
made a little headway owing to a people called the Copts.

We must now go back some few hundred years to the
time when the Israelites were the slaves of the
Egyptians. A Master rose up among them—Moses.
Who was Moses? And how did he form a religion?
Who he was is a question; but he was the most pro-
ficient Master of his time, and, at one time, was the
High Priest of the temple at Sinai, which then was an

Osirian temple. Whatever Moses was, it is known that his wife was an Israelite and that he threw in his lot with the Israelites in all their troubles and adversities contingent with slavery. They elected him their head. He saw the Osirian or the Inspired Religion being debased by idolatry and was determined to save his people from it, so he modified the ancient Osirian religion to suit the then existing surroundings and conditions. The symbols of the attributes of the Deity, he discarded almost entirely, retaining only a few which could not very well be worshipped. He made the worship of one Lord God only—the Deity.

Many of the teachings in the Osirian religion were in the form of questions. These he condensed and put into the form of commands. As for example: Osirian— Have you honored and do you honor your father and mother, et cetera. Moses—Honor your father and your mother, et cetera. There were forty-two questions in the Osirian. Moses turned them into ten commands.

Many readers of the Bible have been nonplussed when they come across the passage where Moses makes a serpent for the people to look upon in the Wilderness. Some claim that it was a touch of idolatry. It was nothing of the kind. Circumstances warranted him in returning to symbolism for the occasion. The symbol— the Serpent—was to concentrate their thoughts on God as the Creator and the Giver of All Good Things.

One of the ceremonies among the Jews was a burnt sacrifice. The Bible tells us that the sons of the *first* man, Adam, offered up burnt sacrifices. Yet among ancient records we find that 60,000,000 of people lost their lives at one time in the same land before sacrifices were commenced.

I never came across the word sacrifice or its equivalent in any of the writings of the First Civilization. The first time I saw the word was in an old Maya book about 5,000 or 6,000 years old in which it says: "And during the night Mu was *sacrificed.*" In the writings of the First Civilization offerings only are mentioned; these offerings consisted generally of fruit, flowers and products of the fields and gardens. These were taken to the temple and placed on an altar specially provided for the ceremony. On the front of this altar were inscribed the Tau and underneath each arm was a double triangle that reads: "Place thine offering upon this altar."

After Mu went down with her 60,000,000 of souls, all the surviving people of the world commemorated her memory in one way or another, some by literature, some by edifices and others by fire in some form. The Quiche Mayas had a fiery house in their religious ceremonies; the Egyptians a fiery tank in theirs; and without doubt burnt sacrifices *in the beginning* was the form the Semites chose. In later years the Jews applied a theology to the ceremony. I wonder if there is a single Jew living today who knows the origin of their burnt sacrifices. I have never yet found one. The Phoenicians, another Semitic race, adopted idolatry and fell so low as to degrade themselves by offering human beings for sacrifice.

Was Moses an Israelite? An Egyptian record would lead one to believe that he was not a pure Israelite. The record I refer to says: "Moses was the son of an Egyptian Princess who afterwards became the great Queen Hatshepsut." Not a word is said about the bullrushes.

As an example of the gross extravagances in symbols and teachings of the Egyptian priesthood I shall take the triad—Osiris, Isis and Horus. Let us see who they were and what was taught from them.

Osiris was a *man* who lived on earth and about whom there are many Egyptian myths. There is also a short authentic history about him, showing that he was a great Master and lived about 22,000 years ago. Isis was the *symbol* of the Creator's female attribute. From this union a son was born called Horus. Isis had a sister called Nephthys and a brother called Set. So that the female attribute of the Creator had *three* members— two females and one male—Isis, Nephthys and Set.

In plain unadorned language the foregoing says: An *earthly man* Osiris marries *a spirit a female attribute of the Creator* Isis and they have a son. But Isis was *only one* forming the *female* attribute of the Creator. The writings of the Motherland say the Creator was Lahun, *two in one, not* four in one.

Can anything more grotesque or atrocious than the foregoing be imagined? Yet this seems to be the theology and teachings of the Egyptian priesthood for a long period in their history—thousands of years. Is it any wonder that they were thrown into the discard? Dozen of other examples could be quoted, but I think this one all sufficient to show the abuses engrafted into their religion.

During the early part of the history of religion in Egypt, such grossness does not appear. As soon as we know anything about her religion we find its theology very complicated and, without question, this complicated theology was the parent of the diabolical abuses which crept into religion later on.

In the early Egyptian religion I find symbolizations ran somewhat parallel with that of the Polynesians. For instance, the marriage of gods. There is, however, this difference. The result of the marriage of Egyptian gods with other gods was only further to complicate theology. With the Polynesians the marriage of gods resulted in phenomena, such as light, sound, et cetera, which is correct, being the workings of the Cosmic Forces. I shall now give some examples both Egyptian and Polynesian.

The Polynesians believe that all that has been created came from the marriage of gods. The first four gods were the Four Great Primary Forces—a name given them during the earth's First Great Civilization. The Polynesians say: "In the beginning there was no light, life or sound in the world. A boundless night called Po enveloped everything, over which Tanaoa (darkness) and Mutu-Hei (silence) reigned supreme. Then the god of light separated from Tanaoa (darkness), fought him and drove him away, and confined him to the night. Then the god Ono (sound) was evolved from Atea (light) and banished silence. From all this struggle was Atauana (dawn) born. Atea (light) married Atauana (dawn) and they created earth, animals and man."

Now let us have a little Egyptian Cosmogony:—
Seb and Tefnut: offspring, the gods: Osiris, Isis, Nephthys, and Set.
Ra and Hathor: offspring, the gods: Shu and Tefnut.
Osiris and Isis: offspring, the god: Horus.

There were also the marriages of the gods and goddesses:

> Amen Ra and Maut.
> Kneph and Sati.
> Ptah and Bast.
> Set and Nephthys.

I have shown what all these gods symbolized, in a short way, in the Pantheon.

THE ISRAELITES IN EGYPT.—While we are on the subject of the Israelites, let us follow them in their Exodus from Egypt.

When the Israelites made their exodus from Egypt, they left Goshen which is a part of the Nile Delta, and, according to Egyptian records (papyrus), they crossed the *"Sea of Reeds"* and passed into Asia. The Sea of Reeds or rushes is situated at one of the mouths of the

Nile. The water is very shallow and most of it can be waded without danger. When they arrived at the Sea of Reeds a submarine earthquake occurred in the Mediterranean Sea off the mouth of the Nile—probably on the gas belt which runs down from Crete and extends under Africa a short distance from the Nile Delta. This quake first drew off the water, leaving the Sea of Reeds dry—the Israelites passed over, the Egyptian army followed. During its passage the returning cataclysmic wave rolled in over the Sea of Reeds overwhelming the Egyptians. A mistranslation evidently occurs in the Bible. The Sea of Reeds was mistaken for the Red Sea. The Red Sea at the point where it is stated the Israelites crossed lies 200 miles from Goshen. The Sea of Reeds joined Goshen. To have crossed the Red Sea, the Israelites would have had to pass through 200 miles of enemy country, with an army in close pursuit, which means that they would have been overtaken and slain.

Pillars: The Israelites when in bondage in Egypt erected two pillars of brick at the entrance of their temples. In the inner part of these temples was the Holy of Holies where only the high priest might enter.

The Hebrews: The word "hebrew" comes from ebber meaning further back. Apparently, the Jews descended from four groups. Two of the tribes entered Palestine about 1375–1350 B. C. Later ten tribes joined them. These came from Egypt about 1200 B. C. or from 150 to 175 years later than the two tribes.

About 953 B. C. the tribes separated, the two seceded and appointed Jeraboam their king. Reaboam was at the time the king of the ten tribes.

Years later, the Assyrians attacked the ten tribes, and history states that the Assyrians destroyed them. Whether or not they were wholly destroyed they disappeared from history and are now spoken of as *"the lost tribes."*

It cannot be conceived that all were put to the sword. Unquestionably some were taken into captivity, and became assimilated with the Assyrians, especially as both were Semites.

The Assyrians in turn were overthrown by the Medes and Persians. What has become of the Assyrians? Among their descendants today, we should, no doubt, find some of the descendants of the ten tribes, but whether there would be any of them with pure Israelitish blood in them is very doubtful.

Still later, the Babylonians conquered the two remaining tribes. These still survive in our Jews of today. They are, however, scattered throughout the world among all nations.

These Jews hold the Feast of the Passover— Why? They are the descendants of the two tribes who were not in Egypt. It was the ten lost tribes that were concerned in the Exodus and consequently the Passover.

Ezra and his associates wrote the Bible. What is known as the Book of Moses was written by them from documents obtained from the ten tribes who were in Egypt. The writings of Moses were partly in Naga and partly in Egyptian. Ezra obtained a slight knowledge of Naga in a Chaldi during the time he was in captivity; but neither Ezra nor any of his associates were Egyptian scholars. Is it any wonder they made so many errors in translating the Egyptian? Yet for all their errors their work was wonderful.

THE RELIGION OF INDIA.—The religion of very ancient India was that of the Motherland, brought there from Mu by the Naacals, a holy brotherhood. These men were taught religion and the Cosmic Sciences in the Motherland and when proficient were sent to the colonial empires to form colleges and perfect the local priesthoods, who in turn taught the people.

About 5,000 years ago, a race of Aryans began to drift down into India from the bleak valleys of the Hindu Koosh and adjoining mountains. Their first settlement was among the Nagas in the Saraswatte Valley. They were just hardy mountaineers, uncouth and uneducated. The Nagas, the most highly educated race in the world, took compassion on them, welcomed them into their schools and colleges, educated and advanced them. The Nagas received them too well for their own good, for, it called from the mountains nearly all who had multiplied there since the destruction of the great Uighur Empire of whom they were descendants. In time these Aryans dominated the whole of the Northern parts of India including their schools and colleges. Thinking they had learnt from the Naacals all there was to be learnt, they proceeded to drive their gentle, kindly instructors out of the country into the snow-capped mountains of the North.

After a period a sect was formed which was called Brahmins who took or usurped the charge of religious teachings. To attain their own ends, they introduced into religion perverted, incomprehensible theologies having all kinds of extravagance. This was the commencement of the downfall of India, which gained impetus as time went on. They introduced caste, commencing with three only. The caste system was extended, until at last the lowest caste was looked upon as untouchables, and for a touch of an untouchable, the receiver of a higher caste must go into a purification before he could be received again by his own people. The result of this was the final step which brought India down from the high position of leading the world in religion, arts and sciences. All that was left were a few embers where at one time was the bright light of a fire representing everything worth-while in life.

Then a great one sprang up among them, a Prince Guatama. He went back to the original teachings of the Sacred Writings. A vast throng followed his teachings and these became the Buddhists. Buddhism was carried throughout the Orient and was the universal religion.

It was only a question of time before a crafty priesthood began its negative work. The Buddhist priesthood of Northern India fell away from the gentle

teacher, Guatama Buddha, and introduced all sorts of
impossible theologies and theories for the sole purpose
of enslaving the people. Only those in the South remained true to Guatama's actual teachings. Today the
center of Buddhism is a little unostentatious temple at
Kandy, in the Central Mountains of Ceylon. But with
all these priestly traps and pitfalls common to religions
today a spark of the truth has been again kindled and
will soon shine throughout the world. Priesthoods and
politicians never have seen nor ever will see "the writing on the wall" until those walls are falling on them
and it becomes too late to escape. This has been the
history of the world for the past 12,000 to 15,000 years.
The people rise and crush the politicians and the Lord,
in *His own way,* weeds his garden.

A U M is an inscription that has baffled scholars
and scientists throughout the world, the Hindus included, for more than 2,300 years. Its import was lost
when the Naacals were driven out of India by the
Brahmins. Many scholars have attempted to fathom its
meaning. None, however, arrived at any satisfactory
conclusions; even the oldest are indefinite. Examples:

Manava dharma Sastra an ancient Hindu book.
Book 2. Sloka 74. "In the beginning the Infinite only
existed called Aditi. In this Infinite dwelt A U M

whose name must precede all prayers and invocations."
Book of Manu, Sloka 77. "The monosyllable
A U M means earth sky and heaven."
I. T. Wheeler, History of India, Vol 2. Page 481
says:

"As regards the three letters A U M little can be
gathered, excepting, that when brought together in the
word A U M they are said by Manu to form a symbol
of the Lord of created things—Brahma."

H. T. Colebrook in *Asiatic Research* says: "According to Noruka which is an ancient glossary of the Vedas
the syllable A U M refers to *every* Deity.

"The Brahmins may reserve for their initiates an
esoteric more ample than that given by Manu."

Noruka must have been reading a Brahminical version of the Vedas, which they stole from the Naacals,
changed it to suit their own vile purposes and then
foisted it on the world as their own writings.

The *Original Vedas* are a Naacal writing. The Naacals acknowledged *One* Deity only. Therefore, when
Noruka mentions *"every* Deity" it shows without the
possibility of contradiction that the Vedas which he
refers to were altered and doctored and were not the
original writings.

A U M conveys identically the same meaning and
conception as the Mysterious Writing and Niven's
Mexican tablet No. 2379. The difference between these
and A U M is in the form of the writing. The Mysterious Writing and the Mexican tablet are in the old

temple esoteric numeral writing. The Hindu A U M is written in alphabetical symbols which reads:

A—Ahau   Masculine—Father

U—   Feminine—Mother—She

M—Mehen   The engendered—The Son—Man

Note: U is here used as the feminine pronoun—She. M would have been used but it would have been confounded with the following M for Mehen.

The Brahmins formed a complicated theology around this conception, introducing a confusion absolutely incomprehensible to the people. It became a wonderful breeder of awe and superstition.

BIBLICAL SYMBOLISMS TAKEN LITERALLY. *Tower of Babel:* The Biblical *Tower of Babel* has been literally taken as a structure of stone or brick. From some old writings, I am brought to believe that it is a purely symbolical term: that "confusion of tongues" is the crux of the legend.

This legend was not written during the life of Mu. It came later, many years later, when ancient history was being recorded again and mankind once more widely populated the earth. It was therefore a product of the New Civilization.

Extravagances in theology and technology in the various temples, colleges and schools were the cause of the "Confusion of tongues" and the whole structure of Religion and Science was the Tower. Each temple had its own terms and words for its theology. Each college and school had its own particular words and terms for its technical teachings. So that no temple or college could understand the teachings of another. All in fact spoke different languages, no one understanding another. This made a "Tower of Confusion," "A Babel of Tongues": so that the name given to the condition was the only one which would adequately describe it.

Today we are running headlong into another such storm, another such confusion of tongues. We have over 100 sects of Christianity, yet there is only one God. Each sect declares all others are in error. They cannot comprehend each other's language. In Mu there were no sects, no theology. All teachings and wording were so simple that the most uncultivated mind could comprehend them. Mu's religious teachings lasted 200,000 years. When the present Tower of Babel comes crashing to the ground, a new structure will arise on its ruins. And that structure will be the simple religion of Mu.

The Flood: The Biblical legend of the Flood is not a myth nor is it symbolical. It has been wrongly described. Those who wrote the Biblical description simply failed to understand the writings of Moses.

There was a flood which destroyed about one half of the earth and all life thereon; but it was not due to a heavy rain. The Flood resulted from magnetic influences.

The Last Magnetic Cataclysm, the Biblical Flood and the Geological Myth, the Glacial Period, are all one and the same thing.

CHAPTER X

THE TWIN SISTERS—RELIGION AND SCIENCE

IN the writings of the earth's *First Great Civilization* it is distinctly shown that the ancients considered religion and science as necessary one to the other. This is shown by their using the same symbols both for religion and science. These symbols, in the early days, were all *geometrical* figures.

Pythagoras, on his return to Athens from Egypt, taught his pupils: "To honor numbers and *geometrical* designs with the name of God."

Whence did these ancients get their geometrical designs of figures? And what induced them to use identically the same figures to teach both religion and science?

On close examination and comparison I find that most of the geometrical figures used may be found in the shape and details of flowers, leaves, et cetera, as the following examples show:

Fig. 1. The Daisy, a circle. Symbolizing the Sun and His Rays.

Fig. 2. The Syringa, a square. Symbolizing the Sacred Four.

Fig. 3. The Lily, a triangle and crossed triangles.

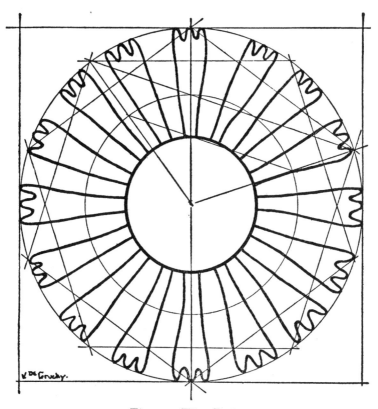

Fig. 1. The Daisy
The Circle—the Sun and her Rays

Fig. 4. The Moonflower, a triangle surmounting a square.

It appears to me irrefutable that the ancients borrowed their patterns of geometrical figures from flowers et cetera. These were nature's creations. Being nature's creations, the ancients did not theorize but followed along the lines laid down by the Creator. They accepted the *Divine Examples* and Laws to follow. In nature the ancient found the highest and finishing school for learning, which calls back a memory of the steps of an old Hindu temple at Lahar, where the great Master said, referring to some wandering jungle minstrels who were playing at the foot of the steps, "Men call them prodigies. There are no prodigies. All things result from natural Laws."

The Egyptians in their early days excelled in Music. "They constructed their instruments to copy the voices of nature."

The old Rishi's parting words: "Go forth into the world, my son, and learn that which is written by nature."

Papyrus Ani. Dated 1320 B. C.: "Behold is it not written in this roll? Read ye, if ye come in the days unborn, if the gods have given you the skill."

The books from which the ancients learnt their lessons are with us today, and at our disposal. Will we learn to read them? Have the gods given us the skill? I shall answer. We have the power to attain the skill. It rests with ourselves to do so.

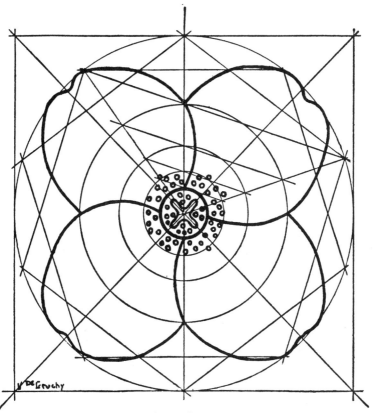

Fig. 2. The Syringa Bush
The Square—the Four Primary Forces

I think the foregoing is sufficient to show that the First Great Civilization obtained its knowledge of religion, arts, and sciences, not by fostering grotesque ideas, mythical theories, theological mirages and mysterious technology, but by studying, copying and applying nature's object lessons that lay before it, and lessons which lie before us today in nature's school of which the Infinite One is the Head Master.

Nature was created and built up on fundamental laws. These Divine Laws have been and are being fully expressed in created objects, all of which have been consistently followed throughout Time. They cannot be impoved upon by man because they are divine. Being divine, they are perfect.

To represent religious and philosophic ideas and conceptions, even of the most abstract order, the ancients employed basic geometric forms as symbols. That they borrowed their knowledge of these geometric forms from natural objects—flowers, leaves and so forth—almost goes without saying. The four drawings of flowers by Viola de Gruchy which were shown at the beginning of this chapter, illustrate strikingly the manner in which the symbols of the ancients occur in nature.

During the past twenty to thirty years, numerous scholars and naturalists have delved deeply into the study of nature's geometry, and with the aid of the light cast by their researches we are beginning to obtain a more just appreciation of the knowledge of the

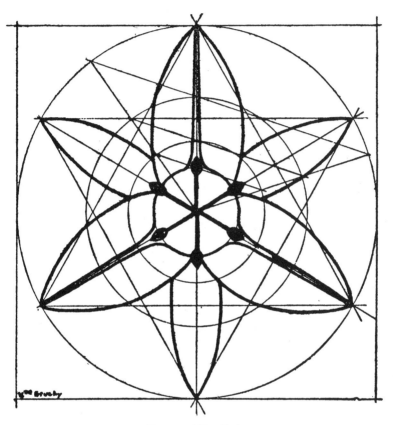

Fig. 3. The Lily
The Triangle—the Symbol of Heaven

ancients and of the extent to which they made practical application of that knowledge in their works of art and science.

A. H. Church (on the relation of Phyllotaxis to Mechanical Laws), T. A. Cook (The Curves of Life) and D'Arcy W. Thompson (On Growth and Form) are but three of the many who have in this century contributed to the rapid development of morphology into an advanced science. And one of the most amazing and valuable results of their researches has been the discovery that the natural laws they reveal were not only understood by the ancients, but applied to an extent unheard of in this civilization of ours, which we too readily accept as the most advanced that has ever graced this earth.

Floral symbols were frequently used by the ancients. Many of these floral symbolizations became myths simply because those of later date of the New Civilization did not comprehend the symbols of the ancients. Something had been forgotten or something was purposely changed for priestly purposes.

As an example and applicable to this work I will quote from: *The Human Side of Plants* by Royal Dixon: "From the earliest history down to the present day, there have been races and individuals who believed implicitly in the spirituality of plants."

"Spirituality is a condition of responsiveness to and membership in the universal spirit of the Creator. The Infinite Substance—God."

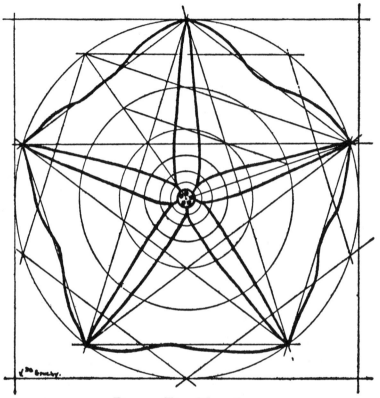

Fig. 4. The Moonflower
The Pentagon—the Full Godhead

THE SACRED SYMBOLS OF MU

"The old Greeks and the Romans gave to the trees and plants the spirits of gods and men: and many more in modern times have lavishly bestowed souls on plants as did Adamson, Bonnet, Hedwig, and Edward Smith —with Martins and Fechner in Germany defending these views and being very liberal in their supply of souls to plants."

"Surely there is a suggestion of some existent truth, which should cause this universal interest and investigation into the possibility of plant spirituality."

In commenting on the foregoing paragraph, I shall say that there is not only a "suggestion" but an "actual truth" which is shown in the ancient writings known and understood by the priesthoods 5,000 years ago and probably only half of that time.

Originally nearly all of the prominent attributes of the Deity had several symbols, or perhaps it would be better to say more than one symbol. A principal symbol for each was either a flower or a tree. Flowers were given the preference for symbolizing Divine Forces and trees for lands and countries. Flowers were very popular to symbolize each of the Four Great Primary Forces. They were also called "the gods," being the command, desire, or will of the Creator. On a few occasions I have found them called "His executive children." These Forces have also prominent geometrical symbols. Take the geometrical symbol and place it on the floral symbol of the gods and it will be seen that the geometrical symbol is on the lines of the sacred flower.

Drawn and analyzed by Viola de Gruchy

In the Greek and Roman myths, it is shown that the ancients used flowers as patterns for the designs of geometrical symbols. The flower was the foundation, the geometrical figure the superstructure: so that by using flowers as symbols for something divine it was quite consistent with the ancient teachings to call these flowers divine, with souls or spirits or whatever the inner self may be for:—The ancients were *not* referring to the flower itself but *to the divine attribute, which it represented in their minds.*

We see this clearly illustrated by the Hindus, Egyptians, Mayas and other ancient peoples where they symbolize Mu the Motherland with a Lotus flower. Times without number, especially in the Egyptian writings, Mu is referred to as "the Lotus"—which was her floral symbol. In these cases, the Egyptians and the others did not refer to the flower, but to what it represented in their minds—*Mu, the Motherland.* Mu was symbolized as a tree, The Tree of Life.

The bronze statue here drawn and analyzed by Miss de Gruchy (see Plate VII) is one of the most ancient bronzes in existence. It is more than 18,000 years old. Its basic design theme is the equilateral triangle, and the skill and rigid consistency with which the whole and its parts are made to adhere to that theme are remarkable.

Is it only a coincidence that the triangle, symbol of Heaven, was employed in the design of this figure representing the Mother Goddess—Mu?

We can take any of the ancient statues, carvings, pictures and designs, found in either India, China, Mexico, Central America, Greece or any other of the old civilizations, and on test it will be found that they all have the foundation of their designs in the first of the Sacred Symbols, prominently the oldest four—the circle, the triangle, the square and the pentagon.

My next and last example will relate to science pure and simple.

We all know that our modern geometry has been handed down to us by Euclid, the ancient Greek. Euclid obtained his knowledge of geometry in Egypt. The Egyptians inherited it from their forefathers who came to Egypt from the Motherland. When the science was fully developed in the Motherland, it is hard to say. In India there are exhibits which show that it was perfected 35,000 years ago. And in the Sacred Writings of Mu 70,000 years old it is shown to be perfected. How far back beyond this last date it goes I do not know. Possibly 100,000 years or more. As examples in geometry I shall take one of Euclid's problems.

First Book—Problem 1. "To describe an equilateral triangle upon a given finite straight line."

The lines of this problem consist of the first two of the Sacred Symbols—the circle and the triangle.

Euclid's works were only one of the dying embers of the earth's First Great Civilization.

Hundreds of other examples might be given involving most of our modern sciences. I think, however, that the foregoing are all sufficient to prove my assertion that during the time of the First Great Civilization which received its death blow with the destruction of Mu, Religion and Science were completely intertwined in their teachings.

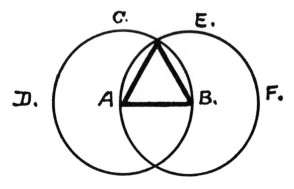

Problem 1.

"To describe an equilateral triangle upon a given finite straight line"

There can be no perfect religion without science: for science unfolds nature, and nature is the mouthpiece which unfolds the Creator and gives the proof of God.

Confucious. 556 B. C.: "Does God speak? The four seasons hold their course, and all things continue to live and grow, yet, tell me, does God speak?"

Were I called upon to deliver a sermon my text would be *Love,* that great *Divine Love* which rules the universe. There would be no hell with its fire of brimstone. For God never made a hell, it is only man's invention and the only hell is what man makes for himself.

THE TWIN SISTERS

"A soul released finds nothing to affright
Save visions false, of terror, bred by creeds,
And deep remorse, that gnaws at evil deeds."

Love is eternal, hell never existed. With the great
Divine Love implanted in the hearts of man all would
be a great brotherhood of Love. This would end all
discord, turmoils and wars among God's family. These
turmoils are with us today, caused by greed, selfishness,
envy, hatred, malice and distrust. These evils could not
be bred or exist if all men were making spiritualism
their primary object in life, and all men worshipped
the Heavenly Father instead of Mammon.

With the Divine Love supreme the lion and the lamb
could lie down together. God Himself is all Love and
is in control of the hearts of man. Without the great
Divine Love chaos, with all of its attendant evils, must
exist. Chaos reigns supreme throughout the world today. Where earthly love exists we see the reflection of
the great Divine Love.

Walking along the jungle paths of the Polynesian
Islands one may meet a company of these children of
the Sun. When passing they accost you with *Koaha-E,*
which means, My love to you. They do not know our
phrases, Good morning, or How do you do. They do
not come in their language for our phrases are of modern civilization and their language comes down to them
from the ancient, but while the words may have become altered the conception remains the same.

If you meet one of the fair daughters of the islands her *Koaha-E* does not invite a flirtation. It is an inherited form of greeting from her ancient forefathers of 12,000 years ago, the time that Mu, her Motherland, sank to form the bottom of the ocean that surrounds her, where the teachings of her forefathers were—Love God and Love One Another.

The ancients in Mu were never taught to fear God. On the contrary, they were taught that the Heavenly Father was all Love and that He could therefore be approached with love and confidence. The ancient religion was based on this. The recent religious teachings have been the reverse of this in general. This condition certainly calls for attention and gives food for thought, that is, for those who are not too busy to think, and for those who are not too egotistical to think. Materialism is responsible for the present chaotic state of the world, if we can believe in the prophecy of Ra Mu at the time Mu was going down into the flames of the underneath. "You shall all die together with your servants and your riches, and from your ashes new nations shall arise. If they forget they are superior, not because of what they put on, but what they put out, a similar fate will befall them."

For the past 12,000 years, since Ra Mu uttered these words, his prophecy has been carried out and will continue to be carried out to the end. How many empires have arisen during the past 12,000 years? Where are they? What has become of them? Why did they fall?

They are gone according to the prophecy of Ra Mu. I now ask—what is going to become of our present civilization?

One of the pearls from the teachings of my dear old friend, the Rishi, which he uttered during one of our conversations was: "My son, the brain of man is his storehouse for knowledge, but the holding capacity of this storehouse is limited. Therefore, never put anything into it that is not valuable for your spiritual progress, or that which is not absolutely necessary for the development and continuance of your material body to the end of this incarnation, in order to prepare for your entrance into the world beyond.

"Learn and store the wisdom of the teachings of nature, for nature is the great school house for attaining wisdom, nature is God's voice speaking.

"Materialism, generally, is not worth storing, only that which appertains to the elevation of your mind and soul, that which will raise you to a higher plane, thus preparing you for the continuance of your life in the world beyond, a step in your eternal life.

"And remember, that when you enter the world beyond, you will leave all materialism behind. You can take nothing with you, nor will you remember anything about it, only Love you will remember, for Love, like your soul, is everlasting, it cannot die.

"Approach the Heavenly Father with full confidence and love. His loving arms are always stretched out to welcome you. If you slip or fall by the way, yet approach Him in confidence and penitence, He will forgive and welcome you because He, Himself, is all Love. The Great Master Jesus explained this in his parable about the return of the prodigal son where he said: 'Joy shall be in Heaven over one sinner that repenteth, more than over ninety and nine just persons which need no repentance.' "

Once again I ask—what is to be the end of this present civilization?